P9-DFD-028

Practical Suggestions for Teaching

edited by Alice Miel

Instructional Approaches to Slow Learning

Practical Suggestions for Teaching

TITLES IN THIS SERIES

From Thinking to Behaving
Louise Berman

Instructional Approaches to Slow Learning
William J. Younie

Social Studies for Understanding
Helen Fisher Darrow

Learning through Movement
Betty Rowen

Reading Improvement in the Junior High School
Deborah Elkins

Phonics and the Teaching of Reading
Dolores Durkin

Independent Activities for Creative Learning
Helen Fisher Darrow and R. Van Allen

Helping Children in Oral Communication
Alberta Munkres

Helping Children Accept Themselves and Others
Helen L. Gillham

Observing and Recording the Behavior of Young Children
Dorothy H. Cohen and Virginia Stern

A Classroom Teacher's Guide to Physical Education
C. Eric Pearson

Building Children's Science Concepts
Mary Sheckles

Individualizing Reading Practices
Alice Miel, Editor

Science Experiences for Elementary Schools
Charles K. Arey

INSTRUCTIONAL APPROACHES TO SLOW LEARNING

WILLIAM J. YOUNIE
Associate Professor of Education
Teachers College, Columbia University

TEACHERS COLLEGE PRESS
Teachers College,
Columbia University, New York

Third Printing, 1970

Library of Congress Catalog Card Number: 67–21694

Printed in the United States of America

Editor's Introduction

Long a classic in the field of slow learning, *Teaching the Slow Learner* by William Featherstone now has a worthy successor in the Practical Suggestions for Teaching Series. William Younie has brought to the subject the results of his own careful analysis together with insights from recent research. He shows the usefulness of distinguishing various kinds of slow learning persons so that their particular educational problems may be approached with more precision. For example, the mentally retarded individual, the one who is emotionally disturbed, and the one who suffers from cultural deprivation may all be slow learners, but each requires something different from the others.

Teachers who specialize in teaching slow learners, those who teach the academically gifted, and those who deal with many kinds of pupils will all be helped by this book to have a better feeling for slow learning children and a better understanding of their teachers' feelings as they try to help them succeed with school tasks.

The author is both realistic and optimistic. There are things to do that will help slow learners not to be underachievers. Administrative arrangements can be made and curriculum adjustments are possible. Professor Younie gives especially practical help in connection with a wide range of subject matter areas, covering both the elementary and secondary levels. In his chapter on educational innovation, the author treats nongraded classes, team teaching, programmed instruction, initial teaching alphabet, work-study programs, and multisensory training. Two appendices contain annotated lists of teaching materials for use with slow learners and a basic reference library for teachers.

Professor Younie has written a comprehensive, interesting, and sound book on slow learning, a "complex problem that affects approximately 20 per cent of those pupils enrolled in kindergarten through grade twelve."

Alice Miel

Contents

INSTRUCTIONAL APPROACHES
TO
SLOW LEARNING

CHAPTER I

Slow Learning and Slow Learners

The children enrolled in the majority of elementary school classrooms in America show great heterogeneity. They exhibit differences in race, color, creed, religion, home backgrounds, physical strength, intelligence, and many other characteristics. Even though this is so, teachers are concerned mainly with differences in behavior and differences in learning ability. This is to be understood, since it is the teacher's obligation to promote learning in the most favorable climate. He is aware that it is his responsibility to disseminate a certain body of knowledge that will assist education in fulfilling its main objective: The child is sent to school to gain information and experience that will help him in adjusting to his environment and that will prepare him to contribute to the development, and thus to the perpetuation, of the society that schools him. The teacher knows that knowledge cannot be imparted properly, unless children are attentive so that they will see and hear what is presented, quiet so that they will not offer unnecessary distractions to each other, polite so that every student has a chance to learn, and orderly so that they may be observed by the teacher (and their learning measured and planned for). Good behavior has many other implications, of course, but all of them are related generally to the reduction of disruptions in the communicative process that must exist between the child and the teacher, the child and the curriculum, the child and the society of the classroom.

The student is usually unaware of the over-all instructional directives and goals that society has set for him. The child's lack of long-range perspective is somewhat to be expected as society has been less than definitive concerning what it wishes the school to teach and how this information is to be imparted. Despite society's uncertainty and his own lack of awareness, the child does know even before he goes to school that behavior and learning are important. Basically, his conception, as gained from his parents and the older children with whom he plays, is that he must be good and he must be smart; and, he will never be smart unless he is good. This conception is reinforced by the teacher who functions on the premise that gross differences in behavior cannot be tolerated if a satisfactory situation for learning is to be established.

The teacher expects to spend considerable time, particularly in the early grades, reducing the span of behavioral differences between the extremes of disruptive actions and exemplary actions. Hopefully, he will build upon patterns that are established and continually reinforced by the home. In the process of reducing extremes of behavior, the teacher will exert most of his effort toward poor behavers in an attempt to move them upward on the behavior scale. This movement will be achieved with various devices, some quite positive, many quite negative.

The young child, too, will be making an effort to adjust to the new experiences of the school. Discussing this, Corey and Herrick [20] * note:

> Frequently for the first time he is faced with the problem of finding out how to win his place in a group. . . . He must accept the fact that school is a place where he has to share his adult world with many other children.
>
> Some boys and girls make this transition from home to school without much difficulty. Others seem to be baffled by what goes on in kindergarten and first grade. They try many bizarre kinds of behavior in an effort to find in this new social environment the same place they had in the circle of the family's affection.

If, after a time to be determined by the tolerance rate of the school system, the poor behavers do not show improvement, their behavior will become one of the characteristics through which they are given primary identification and treatment. This treatment will emphasize the fact that they are different, undesirable, set apart, and generally devalued. The poor behaver eventually may be tolerated only by a teacher, class, or school that has been designated for his kind. In extreme cases, he may be removed entirely from the educational system either for short periods or permanently. On the surface, at least, the teacher usually is successful in placing behavior within specified limits. If he is not, his failure is evident and he also may be asked to leave the school, usually permanently.

The reasons for noticing behavioral differences relate to a concern for the emotional health of each child, for protecting the teacher and

* The bracketed numbers refer to bibliographic references at the end of this book.

children from abusive or destructive students, and for otherwise establishing a satisfactory learning atmosphere. The reasons for noticing learning differences are related directly to the fundamental principles of education and to the basic professional goals of the teacher. There are some educators who feel that the school's concern for behavior overshadows its concern for learning, and thus schools should be founded on the basis of the search for knowledge alone. Schools, such as Summerhill in England that is described by Neill [66], have been founded in response to this feeling. If the school were not concerned with behavior, it could still exist even though it might accomplish very little. However, if there were no concern for learning, the school as an institution would disappear because its purpose for existing would have disappeared.

The concern for learning is so basic that it becomes part of the emotional outlook of the teacher. If a child does well in his studies, the teacher usually takes pride in and accepts credit for this achievement. When the teacher recognizes a bright student, he may offer extra assistance to ensure that the student will develop his full potential. The fact of high achievement is a pleasant and rewarding topic of conversation. It is a topic that is easy to discuss with the student, his parents, and other teachers. Future planning is made more positive for the rapid learner, and he has available to him a variety of educational and vocational opportunities. The high achiever who does not conform to current school or community standards may, of course, be labeled a problem when he exceeds the limits of acceptable behavior. In general, however, nonconformity is more acceptable in the high achiever. In fact, nonconformity may possibly be confused with brightness.

Low achievement is not cultivated or appreciated by society or by its schools. If learning does not reach "normal" levels, the teacher may feel that the child has not been exposed to an advantageous learning situation, is not ready to learn, refuses to learn, or is incapable of learning. Any of the reasons given make the teacher uncomfortable by presenting a direct threat to his professional role. Teachers tend to be measured by the accomplishments of their students, and there is much more reflected glory to be gained from the bright than from the dull. Consequently, lack of achievement has a negative connotation. It is not a topic of comfortable conversation. It is not rewarded by interest and positive attention. And, it is not a characteristic that stimulates positive planning toward future educational and vocational goals. Slow learning is, in general, seen as a problem and as a matter for considerable educational concern. It creates pressures on the teacher that he transfers to the slow student. The poor achiever, unlike the poor behaver, usually remains in school unless his low achievement results in extreme poor behavior. His school presence is tolerated rather than welcomed, and his condition is described as a series of symptoms that the teacher must work hard to treat and overcome.

Slow learning is a complex problem because of the vagueness of its definitions, its high prevalence, and the lack of proved solutions. It cannot be solved by removing the child from the school setting. Since our society considers its schools one of the main instruments for upward social mobility, these institutions, increasingly, have been required to provide for almost all children, including many whose learning needs are not met by the traditional content. If the schools care for the trainable mentally retarded, the involved cerebral palsied, and other students with severe handicaps, how can they excuse themselves from caring for slow learners? However, due to his complexity, the child labeled as a slow learner often is identified but not defined, isolated but not educated, and approached through platitudes rather than through planning. He is treated generally in the public schools as though he were an undefinable enigma rather than an acceptable human being.

THE DEFINITION PROBLEM

The term "slow learning," although widely used, is surprisingly ill defined. When employed by authors and school systems, the term often reflects casual observations of a particular group of learners in a specific school system. Consequently, it cannot be used to generalize a list of standard characteristics or recommended educational procedures. For example, in some large cities, entire schools are designated as being "slow schools" irrespective of the relative intellectual or achievement potential of individual students. In other schools—where college attendance is the rule—the normally achieving child with an intelligence quotient of 110 may be considered to be slow. Or, in schools where a premium is placed on high reading scores, the poor reader may be classified as a slow learner even though his other academic work is satisfactory.

In addition to being formulated from restricted observation, present definitions of slow learning tend to be based on the model of mental retardation that is familiar but not in itself entirely well defined, or, to avoid the issue of specificity, the definitions are based on no model at all. An example of the former approach is that given by Johnson [48], "The slow learners compose the largest group of mentally retarded persons." An example of the more inclusive approach is that used in a curriculum study group [Bolzau and Keltz, 11]:

In order not to get bogged down on the definition of a slow learner . . . the seminar agreed to accept the definition as any pupil slightly below average for whom the multiple curriculum offered in the high school is not suitable and who is not taken care of in the . . . special education program. Since evidence was placed on the positive approach, griping was out.

Another definition problem concerns the decision whether to define slow learning as a constitutional defect or as a functional condition. Some educators prefer to think of slow learning as a static condition and define as slow only those persons who appear to have a hereditary or organic learning problem, which can be programmed for as though it were irreversible. This position leads to the use of terms such as "true slow learner" or "pure slow learner." An increasingly strong position is taken by other educators who insist that no one's intelligence is fixed and that proper manipulation of the learning environment at the correct time can effect positive intellectual growth [Gallagher and Moss, 34; Loretan, 59]. The latter position is summed up by Almy [3]:

Essentially the view of intelligence that I shall present says that intelligence rather than being fixed by genetic factors at birth, emerges as it is nurtured. Each stage of development carries with it possibilities for the acquisition of new abilities, new ways of processing information. Unless each of these abilities is sufficiently exercised as it emerges it will not develop fully and will contribute little if at all to the demands of the next stage.

A precise definition of slow learning is necessary if identification is to have any meaning and if grouping or other administrative measures are to be effective. Yet the recitation of these definition problems leads to one conclusion: There is general agreement that the condition of slow learning exists but very little agreement as to just who the slow learner is. The term "slow learning" adequately describes a global concept but does not serve to define consistently the school functioning of individual learners. The general concept of slow learning includes the implication that intellectual development has been somehow retarded to the point that persons defined as slow learners cannot meet the standard learning expectations of the school. An analysis of various definitions indicates that within this over-all concept a number of different types of learners may be found. Using slow learning as a common prefix, these types may be listed as follows:

1. The slow learner as an underachiever
2. The slow learner as mentally retarded

3. The slow learner as sensorily impaired
4. The slow learner as emotionally disturbed
5. The slow learner as culturally deprived

These various types of slow learners rarely occur in pure form. However, for clarity, it may be useful to consider each of them in isolation so that their similarities and differences may be noted.

THE SLOW LEARNER AS AN UNDERACHIEVER

The underachiever may be defined as a student who is not achieving to his potential intellectual level as determined by objective measures of intelligence. The term assumes further that if the underachiever is given proper assistance he can be expected to achieve as well as others of the same mental and chronological age.

Underachievement arises from many causes and is apparent at all intelligence levels, although it causes the greatest concern with the bright child. Gowan [40] indicates that "practically all gifted children are technically underachievers to some extent" and goes on to describe those who exhibit academic performance that places them more than a full standard deviation below their ability standing in the group having intelligence quotients above 130. Speaking of gifted underachievers, Abraham [1] notes that "They are the undermotivated, underachieving students who tragically add to our educational drop out rate—ability is high; achievement is lower; and aspiration as it relates to the educational future may or may not be high." The gifted underachiever, however, is not generally classified as a slow learner. His potential is usually quite visible and his problem is approached through psychological treatment and intensive teacher guidance rather than through educational adjustments [Wellington and Wellington, 85].

The underachiever of normal ability is often included in groups of slow learners. He may be so grouped deliberately so that he can have the benefit of a special program offering reduced pressure and more individualized instruction. The low achiever of normal ability may also find himself classified as a slow learner, because, despite his intellectual promise, he performs at an academic and mental level that does not indicate his ability. It is recognized that a student who consistently performs poorly in school tasks may eventually perform poorly on intelligence tests, particularly the group type that tend to be correlated highly with academic success. Accordingly, there are some students who look like slow learners only because continued disuse or lack of challenge to their normal intellectual powers has caused them to achieve and to test in the slow learning range. Such underachievers of normal ability are quite prevalent in socially deprived school populations.

Underachievement is not confined to bright or average students. Those with poor intellectual ability may also be underachievers. For example, the mentally retarded generally read below their reading grade expectancy [Kirk, 53].

Underachievement at any intellectual level usually is related to the presence of one or more of the following factors:

1. Lack of challenge or excitement in the learning situation
2. Careless work or study habits developed from an early age
3. Use of slowness to achieve attention that is not given as a reward for more acceptable behavior
4. Failure on the teacher's part to stimulate the child who appears quiet and does not threaten the learning climate
5. Lack of support from the home and environment
6. Poor hearing, speech, sight, and other sensory or physical problems
7. Emotional conflicts of various types and origins

Underachievement can be an aspect of slow learning, but they are not interchangeable terms. The underachiever learns slowly in relation to his tested potential but, even without remediation, he may be capable of performance that is considerably above that usually associated with the term "slow learning." It is important that the underachiever with normal or high potential be distinguished from other types of slow learners, since programs based on the concept of limited intellectual potential, correctly or incorrectly, emphasize a developmental approach geared to limited life goals. These goals are inappropriate for the underachiever with normal or high potential. He should be given a remedial program that emphasizes the achievement of goals similar to those held by the normally achieving child of like intellectual level. An illustration of this programming distinction is given in a policy statement of the "prevocational" (slow learner) program conducted by the Medina, New York Central School [63]:

> In short, our Prevocational Program is planned for those *who* cannot succeed in the regular program, no matter how hard they try. . . . The group of pupils who are underachievers should not be admitted into the Prevocational Program because there is evidence of the possibility of their success in the regular program.

Underachievement is used to indicate a disparity between an individual's actual and predicted academic performance. Its use assumes that the learner's potential, as shown by testing, is accurate and can, in fact, be predicted. These assumptions are tentative at best. Intelligence tests do present a fairly good record of the individual's immediate ability to handle information and concepts similar to those tested. However, all intelligence tests do not sample the same information, and some important intellectual capacities and skills are not included at all in some widely used tests. Also, the tests available do not have the unerring predictive power that would make them so much more useful [Gallagher and Moss, 34]. Therefore, while it is possible within a group of pupils, to identify the underachievers who test within the broad ranges of brightness, normalcy, or slowness, there may be additional underachievers whose potential is not recognized in the testing situation. Hopefully, the classroom climate and methodology used to stimulate those children who appear to have low native ability will motivate the unidentified underachievers to performance levels or testing levels that will reveal their potential.

Although all underachievers could be classified under the global concept of slow learning, the intellectually normal and bright underachievers would not appear suited to long-term assignment to a program designed specifically for low ability students. Since the ensuing discussion is concerned primarily with such programs, no further attention will be given to the bright or normal underachievers.

THE SLOW LEARNER AS MENTALLY RETARDED

Broadly defined, the term "mental retardation" includes approximately 25 per cent of the population of the United States. Technically, a person may be said to have retarded intellectual function if, when administered an individual test of intelligence, he achieves a score between 0 and 85 or 90 [American Association on Mental Deficiency, 4; Terman and Merrill, 79]. The mentally retarded range in ability from a relatively small number of persons requiring complete physical care to a very large group of persons who are generally never considered by the schools to be retarded. The various ranges of retardation are described in a confusion of terms, and usage differs somewhat even between professional groups. For educational purposes, retarded persons are usually grouped by intelligence test scores as follows: borderline, 75–90; educable, 50–75; trainable, 25–50; custodial, 0–25. This type of classification is presently in dispute because it is clear that the great overlapping between groups makes any rigid classification meaningless. And, there is a growing movement to adopt a standard classification system that is independent of the rather arbitrary use of numbers [American Association on Mental Deficiency, 4]. However, the educational classification, as given, still remains in general use.

Despite their technical inclusion in the mentally retarded group, an inclusion that is increasing as the boundaries of retardation are redefined, the borderline students or slow learners are considered somewhat differently from those retarded persons who have lower ranges of intelligence and who are generally not educated or provided for socially in a way that is obviously different from the treatment afforded the general population. Although technically retarded, the slow learner is usually considered in terms that move him closer to the normal population rather than toward the population commonly pictured as mentally retarded. In schools, this feeling is evidenced by the general practice of grouping slow learners in the regular grades instead of placing them in special classes or schools with the educable mentally retarded. Slow learning, in general, is treated as a downward extension of normal intellectual function, rather than an upward extension of mental retardation.

In addition to intelligence test scores, there are other characteristics that distinguish slow learners from other groups of the retarded. One basic difference involves relative levels of academic function. The slow learner is seen as having higher academic potential and being able to handle more complex subject matter. For example, the educable retarded are usually said to have a maximum academic achievement level of fourth or fifth grade. The slow learner is considered to have a potential academic achievement level that is three or more grades higher. Of course, many students in both groups do not reach these projected maximums, and a few exceed them. The slow learner is usually considered to have greater social competence than the educable retarded and is expected to function in adulthood with no social supervision; other retarded groups are increasingly perceived as requiring varying degrees of lifetime social supervision, and to serve their needs many community facilities have been organized. The slow learner usually is able to make his way in the work world without specific help, is expected to be able to hold skilled or semiskilled positions, and is capable of being retrained to meet vocational challenges created by automation and other technological advances. In contrast, although ever-increasing numbers of the mildly retarded are joining the labor force, this accomplishment results from the considerable effort expended by the schools, state vocational rehabilitation agencies, and state employment agencies. The educable retarded, like other workers in low-level occupations, are faced with the threat of unemployment that is generated by a changing technology. However, this group is usually not considered to be a good prospect for the type of retraining programs now available.

Slow learners are also distinguished from other retardates because they lack noticeable physical stigma. While specific facial characteristics and other stigma do not occur to any great extent in the educable mentally retarded, these characteristics are fairly common in other retarded groups. However, the public usually does not distinguish between levels and frequently considers physical stigma to be a distinguishing feature of all mental retardates.

At every level, retardation has been traditionally characterized as permanent and irreversible. This characteristic is increasingly being disputed. One reason for discarding the concept of permanence is that intelligence testing, particularly group testing, is still recognized as being a bit more of an art than a science. There are many examples of changes in individual test scores over a period of time. Also, there is mounting research evidence to indicate that carefully planned preschool programs can increase a so-called retarded person's ability to profit from school experiences and can result in an improvement of intelligence test scores [Kirk, 53].

No method has been devised to determine the exact number or percentage of slow learners who fit the technical classification of mental retardation. Most teachers feel that these individuals constitute one of the largest subgroups of slow learning. They differ from other subgroups in that they do not show any specific innate capacities that would make them suspect as underachievers of normal or bright intelligence; they generally have behavioral characteristics that disallow the label "emotionally disturbed," and they have no obvious sensory defects.

The problem of distinguishing the slow learner who is mentally retarded from the slow learner who is culturally deprived is quite another matter. Few guidelines can be given, except to note that the slow learner who is culturally deprived will usually show a much more highly developed social awareness. This awareness, of course, is evaluated in terms of the child's own culture, not the school's. High performance scores on individual intelligence tests should also alert the examiner to look for cultural problems.

Since the slow learner who is mentally retarded appears to profit from a special program that is free to depart from the traditional instructional practices and content of the school, he is definitely one of the types of slow learners to whom the following chapters apply.

THE SLOW LEARNER AS SENSORIALLY DEPRIVED

Although the sensorially deprived slow learner will be discussed here, it is somewhat rare that such a classification of slow learning will be made or used by a school system. The idea that slow learning may be related to sensory deprivation is relatively new. The term may be applied to those children who have not acquired the sensory experiences necessary to achieve success in initial school tasks. These children exhibit the characteristics of intelligence and home background that would appear to permit them success in school. However, during their formative years, they have been denied sufficient exposure to and practice in those sensory-motor experiences that form the essential base for early school learning. This denial may have been caused by restrictive factors in the environment, or it may be related to slight neurological damage that limits the child's ability to profit fully from the experiences to which he has been exposed.

The classification of sensory deprivation appears to be rarely used because, traditionally, schools do not formally classify children as being slow until after they complete kindergarten or first grade. The postponement of classification reflects the psychometric difficulties inherent in early diagnosis and the fear of stigmatizing the child. Since one of the characteristics of sensory deprivation is that it is clearly noticeable only in the earliest school years, the child who initially could have been described as sensorially deprived is seen at the time of later diagnosis to exhibit characteristics that are identified with more familiar classifications, such as mental retardation, emotional disturbance, or cultural deprivation. Unless the teacher of younger children tests routinely for sensory deprivation as suggested by Kephart [110], the sensorially deprived slow learner may never be correctly classified despite his continuing slowness. One exception to this generalization is the sensorially deprived slow learner who has minimal neurological impairment. Such nonmotor brain damage can result in behavior that is seen to be characteristic of the neurologically impaired, and appropriate educational treatment may be attempted even in the primary grades.

The sensorially deprived slow learner who is not diagnosed and treated early appears to be rather indistinguishable from other types of slow learners. Perhaps, as diagnostic techniques are sharpened and appropriate remedial plans are devised, the sensorially deprived slow learner can be educated in a setting that is ideally suited to his needs. At the present moment, however, the program given to other types of slow learners often must suit the sensorially deprived slow learner as well.

THE SLOW LEARNER AS EMOTIONALLY DISTURBED

Emotional disturbance occurs in many forms. In some of these forms, particularly those that are evidenced by acting out behavior, the disturbance is noticed quite quickly, and steps to alleviate it are initiated; in other forms, particularly withdrawal, the manifested signs appear to mirror poor intellectual functioning and a resulting poor performance in school. The withdrawn child's slowness can, through careful psychological testing and medical observation, often be identified as resulting from an emotional problem. Although not disruptive and therefore not as noticeable, the withdrawn child's behavior should provide the teacher with as many clues to remedial action as the noisy, hyperactive behavior of the aggressive child.

Despite recent progress in sensitizing teachers to the characteristics of a child with behavioral disturbances, some emotional problems that depress the learning rate are still attributed to "laziness," "general immaturity," "stubbornness," "shyness," and other "personality problems": a symphony of symptomatology that is drawn from educational folklore rather than from the lexicon of modern psychology. This situation is particularly true in the early grades where deviant behavior is somewhat easier to tolerate and explain away and where hope is still strong that the child will "outgrow" his learning problems. Because some teachers are not sensitive to emotional problems and since adequate psychological and medical services are not available in all schools, there are an undetermined but possibly large number of children in need of psychological or psychiatric assistance who are treated only for their apparent slowness. The difficulty in diagnosing these children is compounded by the fact that disturbed behavior may result when academic pressure is placed on the slow child who is retarded or sensorially deprived. Thus, the chicken and the egg question is constantly raised: "Is the child slow because he is disturbed or is he disturbed because he is slow?" At present, there is no satisfactory answer, and programming must be organized that will give adequate consideration to both problems.

The pupil who performs poorly in school and is also aggressive or withdrawn must first be considered from the standpoint of his behavioral characteristics; a careful determination of his emotional problems should be made before educational measures are planned. The disturbed child should be diagnosed and prescribed for by behavioral specialists working in concert with the teacher. An informal treatment plan devised by the teacher alone to reduce pressure or provide individual attention may be more harmful to the child than helpful, because it does not consider his over-all problem. Even if the child is obviously slow, as well as disturbed, his placement in a slow group may not be an appropriate solution to either problem, and it may result in the total disruption of an otherwise satisfactory learning situation. School experiences often comprise part of a successful therapy plan for the emotionally disturbed slow learner, but the school itself is not basically a therapeutic institution. And, too often, an educational solution is devised by the school for a problem that is not primarily educational in nature.

The school should not plan for the functionally slow, emotionally disturbed child as a slow learner unless competent psychological, psychiatric, and medical opinion indicates that the child has characteristics and problems that can be best provided for in the slow learner program. Unless the school follows this procedure, the slow learner program can become a dumping ground for all children whose special education needs are not otherwise provided for. It is felt that educational provisions for slow learning should include the subgroup of the emotionally disturbed slow learner only if the behavioral and learning characteristics of specific children within this subgroup complement the learning and behavioral characteristics of other slow learning subgroups.

THE SLOW LEARNER AS CULTURALLY DEPRIVED

The term "cultural deprivation," like its approximate synonyms (social disadvantage, low-socioeconomic status, alienated youth, educationally disadvantaged, and miseducated youth), has certain deficiencies:

1. It describes a sizeable minority of the general population. This minority does not hold the same values as does the majority, and this value difference results in an alienation between the two groups that causes particular conflicts in the school setting.
2. The term can be attacked by members of the majority and minority populations, because it describes the cultural problem inaccurately, demeans the minority population, or is unacceptable for some other reason.

Despite these deficiencies, the term "cultural deprivation" has fairly common usage, has taken on a rather specific meaning, and is as good or as bad as any substitute term presently available. Therefore, "cultural deprivation" will be used throughout the discussion that follows. Those who do not concur with its usage are encouraged to insert their own favorite term.

As mentioned earlier, the definition of slow learning is complicated by the fact that some distinction must be made between low functional performance and low potential performance when planning an educational program. If the child's present poor performance is consistent with the information available concerning past performance or potential ability to perform, he may achieve success in a program that has limited academic objectives and is essentially developmental in character. If the child performs poorly and this performance is not consistent with his past or predicted performance, he may be served best by a program that is oriented toward standard academic goals and is essentially remedial in nature. When the culturally deprived slow learner is considered, it is very difficult to know whether slowness is caused by deprivation (lowered function) or deprivation results from slowness (lowered potential). The difficulty is caused by lack of intellectual measures that truly test potential and compounded by the complex social and emotional feelings associated with cultural deprivation.

In practice, considerable effort is being expended on "culture-free" tests and other measures designed to differentiate potentially slow, culturally deprived students from those with lowered function. Attention is also being given to providing preschool programs, such as Head Start, which are designed to alleviate the deficiencies of deprivation at an early age. Hopefully, this attention will lessen the need for future efforts at differentiation.

At present, the culturally deprived slow learner constitutes the largest slow learning subgroup. A common characteristic of culturally deprived slow learners is their lack of those life experiences that must precede academic learning. The lack of experience and the ability to overcome this deficiency varies widely among individuals. By no means can it be said that all of the culturally deprived are slow learners; nor can it be assumed that all culturally deprived children who function as slow learners will become average or fast learners if they are given special preschool instruction, intensive family casework services, and other enrichment provisions designed to overcome the deprivation that appears to cause their slowness. Apparently, despite a group's cultural or financial level, high or low, it will always have some members who are slower than others. The teacher must plan his program so that the child who appears to be a culturally deprived slow learner will be allowed to find himself. The teacher also must learn to live with the uncertain diagnosis arrived at with present assessment techniques. The teacher may be better prepared to assume both tasks if he has at least a brief knowledge of the so-called deprived culture from which the child comes.

The culturally deprived are found in large numbers in most urban settings. They are found also in suburban and rural areas. The specific reasons for cultural deprivation differ from place to place, and the reactions of the various deprived groups to their circumstances differ also. However, a significant number of the culturally deprived have certain common characteristics from which some tentative generalizations may be drawn.

According to Riessman [103], the culturally deprived child is faced with a number of barriers to learning that, in some cases, result from the school's efforts to assist him. The child feels alienated by unconscious discrimination shown by teachers and other school personnel—discrimination resulting from the fact that the school is a well-developed social agency founded on Christian principles. As such, it holds traditional attitudes toward the poor or "lower classes." These attitudes are often rather patronizing and result in "talking down" to the child, watering down his curriculum to meet lowered expectations, and preconceived planning for predetermined deficiencies that may or may not exist.

The patronizing attitude of the school is often in direct conflict with what the deprived child and his parents perceive as the purpose of education: the economic bettering of the individual. Traditionally, schools have been organized to present a core of learnings related to the more abstract meanings of life. The culturally deprived child brings to school a strong desire to assimilate a core of learnings that have a direct vocational base and can be identified readily with vocational goals. This conflict results in an attitude that the school interprets as a lack of interest in learning. Actually, the deprived child may be quite interested in learning, but he may see little direct value in the traditional offerings of the school. He wishes to learn but on his own terms.

A further point made by Riessman [103] in describing the deprived child is that the social values of his environment differ considerably from those held in the typical "middle-class" school culture. The deprived culture evidences an instability of the family and the labor force and, hence, the pocketbook and the dinner table. The deprived culture does not have the social mobility that accompanies education and the accumulation of wealth. The deprived culture is largely a dependent culture, which cannot escape its dependency but can hate it with the energy that it is not permitted to channel toward the realization of more positive goals. The instability, the immobility, and the frustration have led to:

1. The development of a subcultural language that, although rich in expression and very economical verbally, is grammatically incorrect and a poor foundation for Dick and Jane;
2. The quest for an inflexibility of opinion that appears to be a factor in achieving some matter of stability;
3. The fostering of ideas and behavior patterns that attempt to conserve those experiences that have been tested and found to offer comfort and security;
4. The continuation of family behavior patterns that tend to ensure conformity but do not guarantee progress.

The culturally deprived slow learner must be approached in a manner that allows the school to discover and evaluate his characteristics and affords him the opportunity to discover and accept the values of the school. This approach necessitates the jetisoning of preconceived attitudes toward cultural deprivation and slow learning. Once the functioning level is discovered, it must be challenged through the use of language and situations that are familiar to the child's culture but that are used in a manner that allow him to set goals toward which he wishes to grow. There must be structure, strong motivation to learn, well-organized learning sequences that move carefully from the concrete to the abstract, and imaginative approaches that are based on a careful study of each child and his subculture. These approaches are very similar to those generally promulgated for slow learners, regardless of their cultural background. Thus, the problem of differentiating the slow learner as culturally deprived from other subgroups of slow learners may not be as complex or important as it appears—but only if the entire school recognizes its role in treating learning problems for the deprived and modifies its attitudes and demands, so that such problems may be minimized or eliminated. If these attitudes and demands are not altered, it is doubtful that a program for any type of slow learner can succeed.

DEFINITION SUMMARY

The idea has been expressed that there is a general term, "slow learning," that encompasses several specific types of slow learners. These slow learners may be slow because of inherent defects and/or cerebral damage, or they may only be functioning slowly because of some problem that, hopefully, the school can alleviate. Some slow learners can be given a program of remedial education; others will require a complete restructuring of the traditional curriculum.

It is felt that any definition of slow learning must consider the various types of slow learners in reference to their common learning problems and not merely be based on the observation that they learn more slowly than other children. Thus, within each subgroup that is identified under slow learning, there are those students who can be educated with other types of slow learners and those who must be educated with children who are classified otherwise. The following are examples of this concept as applied to instructional planning.

The underachiever of normal or high intellectual ability learns more slowly than his potential suggests. Yet, this potential places him among other normal or bright learners in terms of criteria other than academic achievement.

Therefore, while the slow learner of normal or high potential requires special counseling, tutoring, psychological help, and other types of attention in order to reach this potential, he will usually be able to achieve best in association with his normal or bright peers.

A slow learner who is diagnosed as emotionally disturbed with normal or bright function may profit academically from temporary placement with slow learners where he may obtain more teacher attention and experience more learning success. Yet the total diagnostic plan may indicate that such placement is a threat to the student's self-concept, thus posing a possible cause of further disturbance. In an instance of this type, the student should be placed in a class with his intellectual peers and be educated as a normal or bright student, not as a slow learner. Behavior permitting, this education should be carried on in a regular class with appropriate supportive therapy. If behavior negates such placement, a special class for the emotionally disturbed should be considered.

The child who learns slowly because of emotional problems, but who is classified as having low potential, may best be educated with other types of slow learners, if his behavior permits such placement. If the behavior is disruptive, placement in a special program for the disturbed is advised.

One of the most persistent problems encountered in defining the slow learner is that of inaccurate or incomplete diagnosis coupled with the labeling of a child without attaching a suitable program to the label. The slow learner is often classified and defined according to the characteristics of the group in which he is found, without reference to any selection criteria other than slowness in academic subjects. When a child is given instruction in school, it is assumed that such instruction is based on a clear understanding of his educational needs and a thorough knowledge of the physical, emotional, and social factors that may affect those needs. Even a cursory study of slow learning will indicate that this assumption is not always justified. It is not unusual to discover that a slow learner in his teens is slow because he has a hearing defect that was not diagnosed until he had reached adolescence; to learn that a sixth-grade child is slow because she has a severe emotional problem that has gone undetected because of the child's shyness; or to find a sixteen-year-old "slow learner" with an I.Q. of 125, who somehow was placed in the slow track and forgotten.

It is suggested that the present unsatisfactory process of classification and definition might be improved by careful application of the concept of maximum correction that attempts to avoid diagnostic and placement errors by insisting that each child with a learning problem be placed within a particular classification—but only after careful steps have been taken to identify and correct all his obvious and not-so-obvious problems.

The concept of maximum correction implies that before a child is labeled as slow he be given all available assistance to assure the best solution possible of the medical, emotional, social, or other problems that adversely affect school performance; the concept further implies that corrective action be taken to resolve any additional problems that are discovered, appear, or recur any time after the classification of slow learning has been made. The usual diagnostic evaluation consists of heart hearing, lung thumping, Snellen eye-chart testing, group intelligence screening, achievement examining, and opinion gathering from teachers and the school nurse. These procedures, hastily administered, are not adequate to formulate a diagnosis of slow learning—to attach a label that can shape an entire lifetime. Maximum correction is a careful, expensive, essential procedure. It requires competent and complete medical, psychological, educational, and environmental diagnosis and treatment. Until such a concept as maximum correction is implemented universally, the definition of the term "slow learner" must remain inexact and unprodutive.

TENTATIVE DEFINITION

It should be clear from the previous discussion that the process of developing a specific, useful definition of slow learning is a confused, complicated matter. Such a quest should end with a definition that contains the following elements:

1. Clarity—The definition should specify just what characteristics identify a slow child. The terms used should be simple and their meanings should be specific.
2. Flexibility—The definition should be based on the fact that there are many reasons for slowness in school subjects.
3. Transferability—The definition should result from a study of the many types of slow learners in the schools and consider the many possible instructional provisions that may meet their needs. Hopefully, the use of these criteria will allow the definition to be applied by most school systems and not limit it to describing what exists as a slow learning group in a few school systems.
4. Specificity—The definition should reflect recognition of the fact that while there are many forms of slowness only certain types may be approached for instruction in the same way.
5. Open endness—The definition must consider the complexity of the conditions considered and the inexactness of available diagnostic tools. Therefore, the definition cannot be said to be static or to define a condition that is always irremediable.

Using these criteria, it may be said that, in general, the slow learner is an individual who achieves in school subjects at a rate and in a manner that causes him to be noticed as an intellectual deviant when compared to normal or bright achievers. He does, however, have sufficient intellectual potential to function as a self-sustaining adult. In specific terms, to be defined as a slow learner, the child should meet the following criteria:

Intelligence. To be classified as slow, the learner must achieve an intelligence quotient within a specified numerical range on several standardized group intelligence tests administered over a period of time, or he must achieve a similar rating on an individual test of intelligence administered by a qualified examiner.

The lower intellectual limit of slow learning as expressed in an intelligence quotient generally is set by the state laws defining mental retardation. The most common minimum is 75, but it may be as low as 70 or as high as 80. The upper limit of slow learning is generally determined by the concept that normal intelligence begins at point 90 on the intelligence scale. Accordingly, as determined by common usage, the slow learner's intelligence quotient range is 75 to 90.

Achievement. To be classified as slow, the learner, in addition to having an intelligence quotient between 75 and 90 (or its local equivilent), will be rated by his teachers as being consistently low in academic achievement and will consistently score below average on standardized tests of academic subject-area achievement.

The level of observed and tested achievement in the slow learner will be approximately 1½ to 2 years behind the academic achievement level expected of children of the same chronological age.

Behavior. The slow learner will be considered to have emotional and social behavior that is generally within the normal range accepted by the school. It is expected that the slow learner may have some symptoms of aberrant behavior associated with school failure. These symptoms are to be accepted within the over-all definition as given here, for it is anticipated that such school-associated behavior will be reduced or will disappear after the child has experienced a suitable program.

Permanence. The general definition of slow learning assumes that it is a problem of long standing that will often persist throughout the child's school life. It is expected that well-planned school programs will increase the learning rate of some children, particularly the culturally deprived, and lead to their consequent reclassification as regular learners. If careful diagnostic and maximum correction procedures are followed before classification, however, most slow learners will continue to function in the manner that such designation implies.

Since the definition of slow learning is central to screening procedures, administrative procedures, and curriculum development, the manner in which such definition is arrived at must remain stable if the group it defines is to remain amenable to instruction. It is the child who must fit the definition. If the definition is made to fit the child, it will soon become unsuited to the purposes for which it has been designed. This reminder is, of course, given for the present only. All of the acceptable limits of a definition of slow learning are based in society. As society changes, it is reasonable to expect that the definition will change. It is quite possible as the complexity of society increases that the child who today is defined as a slow learner may fit the definition of mild mental retardation some years hence. Conversely, if this advanced complexity creates more leisure, more demand for service workers, and a basic change in educational philosophy, a definition of the term "slow learner" may disappear, because such a person will no longer be identified as an impediment to the progress of the normal and the bright. As Featherstone [97] indicated,

> Psychologists have pointed out many times that people cannot be sorted into neat groups labeled "slow learner," "fast learner," and the like with any great precision. . . . Nevertheless, there is a persistent tendency to sort out sheep from goats, and to build up a set of ideas about what is true and not true of the sheep or the goats. The results are often unfortunate. Some highly desirable characteristics of the goats may be overlooked because all goats are supposed to be obnoxious and stubborn, and some undesirable and unfortunate characteristics of the sheep may be unnoticed or condoned because all sheep are supposed to be meek and lovable. All "sheep and goat" classifications of people must be regarded as at best very loose groupings, allowing for much overlapping between groups, and of course taking into account only a few of the characteristics that make up human personality.

CAUSES OF SLOW LEARNING

It is recognized that slow learning results from a number of causative factors, yet no thorough study has ever been conducted of the incidence or specific nature of these factors. Teacher observations and school records do indicate that certain causes appear rather frequently. These common causes of slow learning are listed below in order of the approximate frequency with which they are found.

Environmental Disunity (Cultural Deprivation). The environment to which the child is born is one that is generally alien to the environment in which the school is designed to function. Accordingly, the child is unable to bring to school those experiences upon which the school bases its instructional content and procedures.

Constitutional Slowness. The child is born with mental capacities that place him on the intellectual continuum somewhere between normal function and mild mental retardation. Accordingly, the child is unable to bring to school enough mental capacity to fully perceive and assimilate the experiences offered by the school in the form of instructional content and procedure.

Interrupted Experience. The child is born with normal or superior intellectual capacities but due to malnutrition, severe physical illness, parental neglect, or early placement in a residential institution, he is unable to acquire or to use those experiences that are necessary to meet and sustain the intellectual and academic expectations of the school.

Emotional Shadow. The child is born with normal or superior intellectual capacity but due to emotional problems caused by organic, environmental, or intellectual pressures, he is unable to bring to school enough internal control to organize and profit from the instructional experiences offered him.

Minimal Brain Damage. The child is born with some organic brain damage, or he receives such in infancy. This damage is usually slight, but it prevents the child from perceiving and assimilating school experiences to the full extent of his anticipated capacity. The difficulties in perception are often localized to some specific learning function and accordingly are often seen as a problem of personality rather than organicity.

Sociopathology. The child is born with inferior, normal, or superior intellectual capacity but, due to a combination of emotional and social factors, develops in a way that causes him to reject influences outside himself unless he perceives these experiences as being of immediate benefit to him. Accordingly, the child alternately accepts and rejects the experiences offered by the school in a manner that creates intellectual chaos within the child and causes considerable disruption of the school organization. The child with this type of disorder is usually so alienated that his tenure in school in short.

INCIDENCE

A report of the incidence of any condition is related directly to the manner in which that condition is defined. If a report of the incidence of Asian flu is based on a specific definition that must be substantiated through careful medical techniques, the statistics obtained will differ significantly from a report based on a definition that refers only to the general symptomatology of the disease. Since the definition of slow learning varies widely, a report of its incidence should vary widely also. Surprisingly, this assumption is not supported by a study of the literature. Almost all of those authors writing about the slow learner conclude that the incidence figure stands between 15 and 20 per cent [Abraham, 2; Chidley, 15; Havighurst, 43; Witty, 88; N.E.A., 65]. Some authors do allow some flexibility: "15 to 17 or 18 per cent of the children can be considered slow learners" [Johnson, 48]. Other writers indicate some variance among the population on which they are establishing an incidence: "It is estimated that in every sample of 100 students selected at random from the *elementary schools* of the nation there are at least 20 who must be regarded as slow learners" [N.E.A., 65]. Witty [88] indicates that slow learners constitute 15 to 18 per cent of *class enrollment*. The figure of 18 per cent of the *total school population* is given by Chidley [15]. Havighurst [43] notes, "They have an I.Q. between 75 and 90, as does approximately 20 per cent of the *average population*."

Actually, it would probably be more correct and honest to indicate that an exact incidence of slow learning that would be useful to local school systems is unknown. Theoretically, if the Binet Intelligence Test standardization statistics are used, the projection is 20 per cent [Terman and Merrill, 79]. However, every school system does not have a population that matches the one used for the standardization sample. Also, the intelligence tests used in a particular system may not match exactly the standardization data of the Binet test. The incidence appears to become greater as the child grows older and his problem becomes more apparent. And—the percentages generally used apply to the general population, not the school population.

What to do? Incidence figures might best be ignored but for the fact that they are useful in planning programs for slow learners and in assessing any changes in the numbers of slow learners in the schools. If a school system requires incidence figures, it should set forth its definition, screen the students matching this definition in the total school population or in a selected sample at various grade levels, and arrive at its own result. This method is especially appropriate in school systems that use a computer to keep school records. Other school systems will probably consider the procedure too time consuming and expensive for the return involved, and they will continue to use the general incidence rate of from 15 to 20 per cent.

SUMMARY

Slow learning is a complex problem that affects approximately 20 per cent of those pupils enrolled in kindergarten through grade 12. When the school speaks of the slow learners and groups them for instruction, it generally considers the problem as it relates to function. Individual children may be bright, normal, or dull—or rich or poor—but they are treated in a similar way if their achievement level is low. The concept of programming by functioning level is an administrative necessity. However, it poses certain problems to the teacher, for differences in potential level arise from a variety of causes and the learning problems created by these different causes must be treated in different ways. The slow learner, like the retarded or the gifted, is not a totally scientifically measurable and definable package. Slow learners come in all shapes and sizes although they carry the same label. If the slow learner is approached flexibly with the knowledge that confusion is part of his problem, certain plans of action may be developed for him.

CHAPTER II

Characterization

The concept of slow learning implies that there are no inherent physical, emotional, or social characteristics that set the slow child apart markedly from others with whom he attends school. Only in the intellectual sphere does the slow learner usually possess unique characteristics. Differences clearly are observable in the manner in which slow learners, reason, abstract, gain insight, express themselves creatively, and perform other tasks related to cognition. The many other nonintellectual characteristics often ascribed to the slow learner are usually a reflection of his learned behavior and, like all learned behavior, can be extinguished under suitable conditions. Slow learners are not necessarily withdrawn, nor aggressive, nor eager to please. They need not be discipline problems, lack self confidence, or possess many of the other negative personality traits often ascribed to them. If identifiable groups of slow learners in a school do appear to have more than the usual problems found in other groups, the difficulty may be traced to a school policy of formulating special groups solely to remove problem behavers from the general program. Also, teachers who plan for slower groups in terms of anticipated problem behavior often stimulate the behavior they anticipate.

Any discussion of the slow learner's characteristics should be based on the clear recognition that such discussion is designed to clarify rather than petrify an understanding of these characteristics. The characteristics attributed to the slow learning group will not all be found in any one individual, and, when they are found, they will be present in varying degrees. Certain characteristics, particularly those in the social and behavioral areas, will be more prevalent in certain types of slow learners. The characteristics of an individual slow learner will generally change, for better or worse, as the child's school environment is changed—for better or worse.

In 1941, Featherstone stated:

Comparatively little is known, in a scientific way, about the growth patterns of individual slow learners, but there is evidence to suggest that they have the same quality of uniqueness that one finds in studying the growth pattern of other children.

In the ensuing twenty-five years, we have seen the development of jet propulsion, interplanetary rocketry, atomic energy, computers, automation, transistors, and many other scientific and social advances, including the bikini and monokini, yet little has occurred to date Featherstone's statement.

The present knowledge of the slow learner's characteristics is based largely on a few small group studies of variously defined slow learners and a great number of general statements made by teachers and others who work with slow learners. Each of the studies and personal reports is, in itself, inconclusive. However, when taken as a group, they present a tentative picture of the slow learner that must suffice until more precise information is available.

In closing this preamble to a discussion of characteristics, it must be said that a careful study of an individual slow learner will reveal few surprises. He exhibits the same types of behavior with the same frequency as any other child. He should be studied always with reference to his more intellectually normal peers and should not be isolated as being a terribly special type of individual.

MENTAL ABILITIES

Generally, the most noticeable characteristic of the slow learner is a lowered rate of mental development and function. The slow learner is not intellectually prepared to learn home or school tasks at the time these tasks are usually introduced. And, even when he has acquired the experience necessary to approach a task, he learns it at a slower rate. In describing slow learners, Johnson [48] notes:

At any specified age they should, on an average, be expected to be performing at from three-fourths to nine-tenths the level of the normal child. This does not mean that they can perform a fraction less of the *same* tasks expected of normal children who are their chronological peers. It means they are actually capable of performing at a fraction less or on a lower level than that group.

The slow rate of learning is not particularly vexing to the young slow learner, but, as he grows older, the rate of learning becomes hopelessly inadequate to cope with the cumulative mass of material that must be learned.

One of the prime elements in the slow child's learning deficiency is that he has more than normal difficulty in making associations. Since a great deal of learning is based on experience, a person faces a formidable handicap if he is unable to relate one experience to another and draw inferences from these relationships.

A reduced ability to make abstractions is another characteristic of the slow learner's thought processes. He often acts upon information that is immediately available, without recognizing its present or future implications. He finds it difficult to learn from material that lacks familiar elements, even though the content includes many clues to ideas he has mastered. He has difficulty questioning ideas and situations because of an impaired ability for discovering the existing gaps in his own knowledge and because of his inability to construct an over-all conclusion from smaller pieces of information. As a result of his abstraction difficulties, the slow learner appears to be an impulsive decision maker, seems to be easily led, and apparently gains very little assistance from the well-intentioned but often abstract suggestions of his teachers.

A person who has difficulty abstracting and associating the information he receives is not too likely to seek additional information. This is so either because he is unaware of this information's existence, or he is afraid of overtaxing an already strained information-retrieval system. Understandably, the slow learner tends to lack intellectual curiosity and shows little interest in exploring any but the most necessary avenues of intellectual contact. In school, he chooses reading materials similar to those that have given him success in the past; he prefers to work and rework familiar arithmetic problems; and, generally, he does not seek new ideas, new procedures, or new activities—although he may react quite favorably to them when they are introduced—so as to minimize the elements suggestive of intellectual challenge. The slow learner is aware that a challenge may simply be another invitation to failure.

When the slow learner does become curious and investigates his environment, he tends to observe without making generalizations concerning what he sees—a characteristic related to reduced associative and abstractive abilities. His slow reaction time also contributes to this problem since he may be faced with more stimuli than he can assimilate in the time provided. How many teachers can wait until the slow child brings himself to respond to what they are presenting? Who has time to give a student clues from which he can begin to build generalizations, when it is much faster to make the generalizations for him? And, where outside of the school does the child have an opportunity to generalize in a world replete with communications media that present pregeneralized information?

Everyone knows that the slow learner has a short attention span. What frequently is not known is that this bit of knowledge tends to keep the attention span much shorter than it might be. The attention span of the younger slow learner is appropriately short, in keeping with his mental age. The attention span of the older slow learner appears to be short because attention depends on interest, and he finds little in the classroom to interest him. When slow learners participate in social and athletic activities or become involved in interestingly presented school tasks, they are not bound by the fifteen- or twenty-minute interest span that has become a standard recommendation when planning for slow learners. When the slow learner, particularly the older pupil, refuses to attend for more than fifteen or twenty minutes, there is strong indication that the material being presented does not merit longer attention or that the child has been taught to believe that all activities are of short duration. It is impossible to say that slow learners should be able to pay attention for any specified length of time. The interest-provoking power of any activity will vary from pupil to pupil. The conditions in the room, the attitude of the teacher, what the child did or didn't have for breakfast, and many other factors affect attentive ability. Also, there are no standards as to just what constitutes a normal attention span for anyone, fast or slow. In fact, it is much more difficult to determine when a normal child ceases to attend, for he has learned early how to daydream and otherwise intellectualize his lack of interest. The slow learner, however, tends to express his need for a change in activity through action and verbalization that clearly indicates when the limit of interest has been reached.

Poor retention of ideas is another often quoted mental characteristic that bears careful scrutiny. There is reason to believe that the rate of forgetting in slow learners and other students could be reduced considerably if more attention were given to presenting meaningful material in an interesting manner.

Using this brief summary of mental characteristics only as a general guide, the teacher should plan to observe his slow learners and give particular attention to discovering how they think and learn. This observation should be continuous and should include comparisons to normal and fast learners. An effective way to determine instructional needs is to plan activities that involve children in a variety of structured and unstructured situations wherein the teacher acts as observer and diagnostician. Teaching that is not based on such careful observation cannot pretend to be efficient or effective. As the teacher observes, he will become aware that each intellectual characteristic tends to suggest the use of an instructional strategy. A few of these strategies are presented below. A more specific application of them is given in the later discussion on methodological approaches.

Multisensory Approach. Learning is dependent upon perceiving, receiving, and translating information from the body's various sense organs. The slow learner's impaired intellectual function frequently is related to a breakdown in this perception-reception-translation process. This breakdown may be due to some defect or lack of development in his sensory apparatus. This defect may be caused by organic damage or environmental interference. The multisensory approach attempts to present ideas in a way that will allow the student to learn through all of his senses, thus bypassing those that may be inoperative or functioning poorly. The multisensory approach also takes note of the fact that all persons tend to have a sense learning preference; that is, some persons learn better by seeing, others by listening, others by manipulating a material, and so forth. The multisensory approach allows each child to use consistently that sense through which he learns best. In practice, the multisensory approach involves listening to an idea, reading about it, making an object related to it, talking about it, visiting its source, and engaging in other activities that will give the one idea the maximum possible sensory reinforcement.

Re-presentation with Variety. The extended learning period that is characteristic of the slow learner requires that the same information be re-presented a number of times before it is learned. Re-presentation can only be effective, however, if the child is consistently attending to the material. Therefore, ideas must be re-presented in a variety of interesting ways. Re-presentation can be varied by including the information to be learned in various subject contexts, by having it presented by different persons (the teacher, a student, a visitor), by using several instructional media, or by other means that repeat an idea while maintaining interest. The impact of each experience is much more important than the number of times an idea is re-presented.

Concreteness with Training in Abstraction. Concreteness is a teaching strategy that suggests itself even after the most casual study of the slow student. It is a strategy that is recommended by all of the books and articles on slow learning, and it is probably the most used teaching technique applied to slow groups. The insistence upon concreteness, however, often solidifies the teacher's methodology to the point that slower students are constantly fed with simple, sterile material that interests neither student nor teacher.

Although an essential concept of instruction, the direct simple presentation of material must be accompanied by approaches that allow the child gradually to develop insights and to perform abstractions that evolve logically from the initial concreteness. There is some research evidence to suggest that specific training in abstract thinking is possible and may result in increased intelligence test scores [Boger, 92]. As the student grows older, he has an increasing need for materials that interpret the abstractions of his social environment. If the need is poorly met through a perpetuation of concreteness, the student will have the choice of accepting the materials presented and extending his immaturity, or the self-destructive, escape activities that are the choice of so many who feel that the school has very little to offer.

These few strategies are presented as examples of how knowledge of the slow learner's mental characteristics may be applied to everyday programming. As the teacher builds specific knowledge of the mental characteristics of his slow learners, additional strategies should be developed.

PHYSICAL CHARACTERISTICS

When the slow learner's physical characteristics and capabilities are enumerated, he appears to be only slightly deviant from the norm. Most authors describe slow learners to be somewhat shorter and lighter than average for their age. Slow students have more minor physical defects than does the general population, and they are more prone to infectious diseases.

Although no research evidence is available to support these general descriptions of lowered physical capacity, they tend to be confirmed by studies with the gifted and the retarded. These studies show some positive correlation between level of intelligence and physical size, physical ability, physical attractiveness. Until specific data is available from studies that report the physical characteristics of a large representative group of slow learners, the use of available information must be tempered by the knowledge that it may reflect only the characteristics of the culturally deprived subgroup. The deprived slow learner—like the majority of deprived persons—is often ill-nourished, has not received adequate medical care, and is exposed to disease-breeding conditions.

The slow learner's physical characteristics are probably slightly below average, but this supposition does not appear to affect his athletic ability. Since slow learners do possess nearly normal physical attributes, they can function adequately as athletes if the required tasks are defined in simple terms and the necessity for decisions is limited or can be outlined in advance. Slow learners often find considerable self-satisfaction and success in athletics, where their performance is measured in purely physical terms. Their success can frequently be carried over to the classroom. Unfortunately, this approach to learning through physical activity is denied to many slow learners by schools that predicate participation on athletic teams upon a standard point average in academic subjects.

The physical characteristics associated with slow learning indicate that the teacher should consider the following suggestions in planning his classroom routine:

1. There is need for extreme alertness to physical defects that may affect learning. These defects, particularly if minor, probably will not be noticed or provided for except in school.
2. An awareness must be maintained of any changes in the child's environment that may affect his general health or physical vitality.
3. Specific attention should be given to developing general physical abilities such as eye-hand coordination.
4. Students should be provided with opportunities to participate in physical activities such as athletics or crafts; success in these may prove to motivate the student toward academic and social development.

PERSONAL ADJUSTMENT CHARACTERISTICS

The slow learner is generally devalued by a society that places a premium on intelligence and education. Recognizing his devaluation, the slow learner frequently develops personal attitudes that deny education, or accept it at a very superficial level. The slow child's resultant concept of himself as a learner may be so damaged that, even when he is given competent instruction, he chooses to fail because this is a role he understands and anticipates.

The slow learner's difficulty in developing an adequate concept of himself as a learner results in a generally unrewarding pattern of personal adjustment. He is often seen as lacking in initiative, having fixed opinions, and exhibiting other personality characteristics that may be described as rigid and defensive. The slow student has a limited sense of humor, has considerable difficulty expressing himself in formal language, and may have poor personal habits that increase rejection by his peers. This personality description, of course, varies from learner to learner. Generally, it cannot be ascribed to slow learners of primary school age or those who have received the benefits of a well-planned educational program.

The personal adjustment characteristics of the slow learner suggest that the teacher should spend considerable time helping this child develop an adequate self-concept. Attention must be given to how the child feels about himself and how the feelings affect his school performance. This activity will have more likelihood of being successful if the teacher has a knowledge of basic guidance and counseling techniques and has the assistance of a psychology and guidance staff. Humor is useful in dealing with slow learners as long as it is not directed at the learner and allows him to release tension in acceptable ways.

Since one of the personal adjustment problems of the slow student is that he is not always certain of the value that school activities have for him, he requires opportunities for constant reassessment of his instructional progress through active involvement in the evaluation process.

The slow child's learning problems cannot be divorced from the personal problems they tend to create. The teacher who devotes time to understanding the child's personal characteristics and problems has a distinct advantage over the teacher who focuses on instruction alone.

SOCIAL ADJUSTMENT CHARACTERISTICS

The over-all social adjustment picture of the slow learner is that of a child who has the same potential to adjust to his social environment as any other. However, the slow learner has fewer social contacts, especially in the school, where his social mobility is restricted because of his learning problems and devaluation by peers. The slow learner's reactions to his isolation tend to place a greater distance between him and his social environment. Not surprisingly, then, the slow learner represents the largest number of school truancies and dropouts, and he is frequently listed among those juveniles charged with delinquency.

The poor social behavior of the total slow learning group may be an overgeneralization from the subgroup of culturally deprived slow learners—as delinquency and crime rates for groups from deprived areas are higher than in the general population. The slow pupil's poor social record may also result from the fact that he bears a label that carries a certain expectation of delinquency. The slow learner's inability to abstract and generalize may lead him to follow delinquent leadership. Or, his basic slowness may result in his being caught more often than the normal or bright delinquent.

These speculative reasons for the slow learner's generally inadequate social adjustment may be helpful in seeking solutions, although it appears that the most pressing area for investigation has not, as yet, been mentioned. The school—in its inability to accept the slow learner and through its general unwillingness to plan an adequate program for him—may be the root-cause of the slow learner's poor social adjustment. The school is not responsible for the poor homes or neighborhoods in which many slow learners live. It is not totally responsible for the changing social climate that appears to result in more delinquency at all intellectual levels. Yet, the school is the force through which the slow learner and his family may realize their social expectations and achieve social mobility. The school does have the responsibility of providing the specific assistance needed if the slow learner is to achieve these goals. The social-adjustment characteristics of the slow learner suggest that the teacher should attempt to:

1. Plan school activities from the child's environmental base, neither rejecting it because it is different from the teacher's own, nor perpetuating it because it is the only experience the child has had.
2. Involve the slow learner's family in all educational and vocational planning to ensure that the school's expectations will not be in disharmony with those of the family.
3. Give the child many opportunities for reality testing that are accompanied with interpretation and positive reinforcement.
4. Provide a forum for group and individual discussion of social adjustment problems.
5. Assist administrators, teachers, and pupils to understand the slow learner and to provide him with adequate educational programs.

CHARACTERISTICS SUMMARY

The preceding review of the characteristics of the slow learner is rather general and provides few definite answers to the teacher's immediate classroom problems. What information, then, do we glean from this or any similar review of the slow learner's characteristics?

1. The review indicates that the data available are quite inadequate. Answers to the following questions must be forthcoming.

At what level in the school are specific characteristics of the slow learner identified?

The answer to this question would tend to tell us what characteristics the slow learner brings to school and what characteristics are imposed on him after he arrives.

How fixed are the mental characteristics commonly associated with slow learning?

If mental characteristics are fixed, they should be supported by giving the child concrete experiences. This approach is the traditional one for slow learners and is designed to reduce frustration. It also reduces the types of experiences available. If characteristics are not fixed, there is need to provide a carefully designed program to develop reasoning, abstract ability, associative ability, and the like. This program may differ considerably from those traditionally offered in the public schools.

What is the effect of various programs upon the development of the slow child's self-concept?

There has been considerable concern for program content and ways to teach it. Little attention, however, has been given to how this activity affects the slow learner's feeling about himself.

2. The review indicates that characteristics for the total slow learning group have been generalized from one or another of the subgroups. The constant mention in the literature of poor homes, poor communities, and limited experiences provides a strong clue that this overgeneralization may be true.
3. There may be too great a concern for the special nature of the slow learner. "Normal" children also have problems in school.
4. The review indicates that very little is known about the slow learning adult except that he may be a dropout or social offender. There is need to know what happens to the slow learner after he leaves school. How does he adjust? What effect, if any, has his schooling had on him? Are his children slow learners? These and other questions must be asked—and answered.

Any characterization of the slow learner has to be made with care. There is a necessity to be prepared in general for the quirks of the slow learner, but there is a need also to be prepared to stimulate and enjoy the positive surprises in his behavior and achievement.

CHAPTER III

Evaluation

The educational evaluation of slow learners is a continuous process. It should begin when the child is referred for possible identification as a slow learner and end with evaluation for vocational placement. Complete and thorough evaluation procedures in slow learning are essential to planning individual programs of education. They are vital also as the basis of general administrative and curriculum planning.

IDENTIFICATION PROCEDURE

The identification procedures used by a school system to discover slow learners will depend on several factors. These include the relative sophistication of the school's over-all evaluation plan, the availability of psychological and guidance services, and instructional provisions that are in effect for the slow child.

The prime instrument in any identification procedure is the teacher. His observations and referral begin the identification process. He supplies the information and opinion that are crucial to the eventual diagnosis. One of the teacher's traditional and most obvious methods of identifying slow learners is to compare a child's chronological age with his grade placement. Usually, the child who is more than two years overage for his grade may be considered a possible slow learner. The final decision as to his slowness depends upon an analysis of why he is overage. Did he begin school late? Has he had a severe illness? Has he moved a great deal during his early school years? Attention must also be given to more formal diagnostic procedures. Obviously this method is not appropriate until grade three or four, and it cannot be used in the increasing number of school systems that, as a matter of policy, do not permit more than one or two retentions during the student's school career.

The teacher is more likely to identify possible slow learners through information gathered from achievement tests and group intelligence tests. In some instances, he also may have available the results of an individual intelligence test.

Achievement Testing. The achievement test is frequently used to help identify slow learners. The suspicion of slow learning usually is confirmed if the student's achievement test scores are two or more years below the grade level expected of his age and all of the following conditions are met:

1. The lack of achievement must be general and not limited to one or two academic subjects.
2. The achievement test scores must be equal or inferior to the performance reported on intelligence tests.
3. All circumstances that might lower results of achievement or intelligence tests must be investigated and eliminated as possible sources of test interference.
4. Achievement test results must be measured against the quality of instruction. In some schools, the level of instruction is so low that almost all children achieve below expected grade levels.

Achievement testing becomes an important element of the identification procedure at grades two or three. Before that time, academic readiness test or reading test results may be used as a general guide to diagnosis, since the child's other academic experiences have been rather limited. At whatever level achievement tests are used, it is important that they be selected with reference to the child's ability to handle testing situations. The object of achievement testing is to test achievement, not to determine how well a student follows complicated test directions or how quickly he fills in blanks and spaces that are located in impossible places.

There are no reliable ways of determining what is the most effective achievement test for a particular school except by carefully examining several tests and actually using them with slow students. Most school systems have adopted achievement tests for systemwide use but will allow the occasional use of other tests that appear to be more suited for the identification of certain types of problem learners.

Several general achievement tests that have been listed in the literature on slow learning and mental retardation are: *

* This compilation and others presented here are intended to give teachers a starting point in their quest for suitable tests. The listing of any test does not imply recommendation. In a specific situation, tests not listed may be equally or more effective than these tests noted. For comparative data on a variety of tests, the reader is referred to: Oscar Krisen Buros (ed.), *The Sixth Mental Measurements Yearbook*, Highland Park, New Jersey: The Gryphon Press, 1965.

California Achievement
Gray-Votaw-Rogers General Achievement
Iowa Tests of Educational Development (Grades 9–12)
Metropolitan Achievement
Sequential Tests of Educational Progress
Wide Range Achievement

Although not classified specifically as achievement tests, there are several tests of language ability that may be included in the procedure for diagnosing slow learning. Perhaps the best known of these tests is: The Illinois Test of Psycholinguistic Ability (ITPA).

Group Intelligence Testing. Probably no other evaluation instrument is as important or as misused as the group intelligence test. Group intelligence tests indicate the comparative level of the child's present intellectual function and are most useful in evaluating his present capacity to perform school-designed academic tasks. Group intelligence tests are not useful in predicting future intellectual performance. They are best used as a rough screening device to discover those pupils who require intensive diagnostic attention. The results of group intelligence tests should not be the sole criterion for grouping, for determining grade placements, for planning remedial instruction, or for family guidance.

The group intelligence test score is subject to relatively large errors, as it may be heavily dependent upon reading skills, is usually administered by a relatively untrained examiner, is generally administered in a classroom (a setting that is less than ideal as a test environment), and provides no record of the process the student used to achieve his test results. The intelligence quotient attained on a group intelligence test is a pure number and, like all pure numbers, has very little meaning in and of itself. It must be related very carefully to the child's achievement, personality, environment, and numerous other factors, before it becomes useful.

As with achievement tests, school systems usually do not leave the selection of group intelligence tests to teachers. However, if the teacher has an opportunity to select a test for specific use in identifying slow learners, he should be certain the test content and format is appropriate to the child's reading and social level.

The following group intelligence tests have been reported as being used with slow learners. They are listed in alphabetical order and are only representative of a number of similar tests.

California Test of Mental Maturity
California Test of Mental Maturity: Short Form
Henmon-Nelson Tests of Mental Ability

Kuhlmann-Anderson Intelligence Tests: Seventh Edition
Lorge-Thorndike Intelligence Tests
Otis Group Intelligence Scale
Otis Quick-Scoring Mental Ability Tests
Pintner General Ability Tests
(Two Series: Nonlanguage Series; and Verbal Series)
Terman-McNemar Test of Mental Ability

Individual Intelligence Testing. The test of individual intelligence is more reliable than the group intelligence test. However, the individual test is not an ideal instrument and is not yet at a stage of development that allows its results to be used indiscriminately. Individual test scores reflect present intellectual function only. They are not predictive, and their results can be used as a guideline—not as a prescription.

An individual intelligence test is administered by a qualified psychological examiner. He usually spends an hour or more giving the test and two or more hours studying and reporting its results. The administration of individual intelligence tests is expensive and time consuming, and they are not used routinely to identify slow learners except by schools that have well-developed programs for slow learners.

When individual tests cannot be given, it is recommended that two or more group tests be administered. The results should be compared with one another and with any group intelligence test scores that appear in the child's record, providing, of course, that the various scores are comparable. Scores achieved on a nonverbal test do not relate to school success as well as those earned on a verbal test. Consequently, verbal and nonverbal test scores are not comparable. Some tests cannot be compared because their timing schemes differ. Also, different tests may be sampling different abilities and thus may not be comparable. The best way to avoid any question of the comparability of specific group intelligence tests is to have them chosen by a psychologist familiar with test construction and selection.

Other Identification Techniques. Identification of the slow learner should include a thorough medical examination, a complete review of his past school record, a complete consideration of the conditions in his home and neighborhood, a measure of his social development, and a complete survey of his emotional health. As noted in the previous reference to maximum correction, the slow learner should not be so labeled until all completed diagnostic and remedial procedures point to such a designation.

General Guidelines. Identification of the slow learner should be a by-product of a continuous effort on the school's part to discover learning problems in its pupil population. Identification should not be a response only to the steady referral of "problem" children. The general school-population screening should be followed by a fine analysis of those students who appear to be educational problems. If at all possible, the fine-screening stage should include individual intelligence testing and use of special techniques designed to discover sensory, physical, or intellectual defects that may contribute to the learning deficit. It should not be inferred that the identification process will be limited to formal tests and procedures. The careful use of guidance records, report cards, anecdotal records, and other material is essential to a complete evaluation of slow learning. A study of the past school history is particularly useful in diagnosing behavior problems, minimal neurological damage, or underachievement.

Identification should be only the first step in a complete educational program. Diagnostic procedures often become highly efficient without a corresponding improvement in the services prescribed for the child. A strong identification program that exists in an educational vacuum will produce little but frustration in teachers, pupils, and parents. From this statement, it must not be concluded that schools should maintain slow classes into which the slow child is placed as soon as he is identified. Quite the contrary is true. A diagnosis of slow learning, especially if made early in kindergarten or first grade, should alert the teacher to the fact that he has a child who needs special assistance. If this assistance is swift and adequate, it is quite possible that later evaluation will reveal that the problem of slowness has been overcome. It is late diagnosis and poor school programs that produce slow learners who can be educated only in a special setting.

The over-all educational plan for the slow learner should include a careful interpretation of all pertinent screening results to the child's teacher and parents. Identification results should be presented in terms of their meaning in a classroom situation, and they should be couched in language that does not require medical or psychological interpretation. When the teacher relates diagnostic information to parents, he must avoid stargazing and deprecation.

Finally, it should be remembered that the evaluation instruments and procedures in common use do determine in a fairly gross way the manner in which a child functions intellectually, physically, emotionally, and socially. They do not provide exact information on the child's specific deficits or how these deficits affect learning and performance. How, for example, is it known if the child has ever experienced an orange and what value such experience might have to him? If given the experience of an orange, will he be able to use the knowledge gained to build the color concept of orange, the spatial concept of round, the taste concept of sweet, the olfactory concept of sharp, the motion concept of roll, and so forth? Or, must he be provided with ways of experiencing an orange that will assist him in building each concept separately and help him in transferring what he has learned to situations containing similar elements? The answers probably will not come from tests but can come from carefully planned curriculum procedures that in the early years explore with the child every conceivable phase of his development.

REASSESSMENT

The initial identification of the child as a slow learner should be a carefully planned procedure but must not represent the school's only effort at evaluation. The needs and progress of the slow learner should be reassessed at regular intervals. If the child remains in a heterogeneous group, this reassessment will take place as part of the school's routine testing program. The only special concern shown for the slow child might be the provision of a test form that is suited to his performance level. Slow learners who are educated in special programs can be given a more thorough testing schedule. This schedule will include the evaluation of achievement. In addition, it will stress procedures that produce detailed diagnostic information for use in planning remedial instruction. Special programs in the primary and intermediate grades should institute a particularly vigilant evaluation procedure. This will assure the proper disposition of those children who evidence the capacity for success in the regular program.

VOCATIONAL EVALUATION

A very important phase of the evaluation program is the assessment of the high school student's vocational interests and potential. This phase will depend more on teacher observations and reports from part-time employers, than on more formal procedures, although some test results are helpful. The results of vocational interest tests may be used for discussion purposes, particularly if they indicate unrealistic aspirations. Vocational aptitude tests are not especially predictive with slow learners but may indicate areas of general weakness that can be remedied while the student is still in school.

The most effective vocational evaluation procedure is the school-work study program. Here, the slow learner has an opportunity to sample various jobs that interest him. His aptitude is evaluated directly through actual work tasks and the observations of a job supervisor. The school work-study program also ensures active student involvement in the evaluation process. Although the parents' influence tends to be less apparent in the later school years, it still has a dominant effect on the student's choices, and, therefore, parents must be included in the vocational evaluation process, particularly when the assessment of vocational interests is the topic under consideration.

EVALUATION SUMMARY

Evaluation of the slow learner is related closely to the over-all evaluation procedures adopted by the school. There are no special tests for slow learners, but some tests may be more appropriate to his needs —and this fact should be reflected in the school's testing policy. The identification of slow learners should be systematic and should be provided for as early in the school years as present evaluation procedures permit. Identification should have a definite purpose and be an integral part of a total school plan for slow learning. This plan should include a definite reassessment procedure that is tailored to the needs of slow learners at different school levels. The final phase of the evaluation sequence should include formal and informal vocational assessment procedures, preferably the real-life testing situation provided by the school work-study program.

At present, evaluation procedures are somewhat crude and often result in an erroneous diagnosis of slow learning or the placement of students in school programs ill-suited to their needs. Testing and observation techniques must be improved, but even more important is the need to improve the way in which evaluation results are interpreted and applied. Evaluation too often is seen as providing a final answer. Actually, it provides but a first clue.

CHAPTER IV

Administration

The administrative approaches to slow learning are determined primarily by the daily administrative decisions made for all children in a particular school system or school. Few, if any, special administrative procedures are developed in response to the slow student's specific learning needs. Accordingly, the teacher may feel limited in his ability to effect specific administrative changes favorable to the slow learner; he may become resigned to working within a framework that is imposed from above. The development of such an attitude would be a grave mistake. While the teacher cannot usually effect direct administrative changes, he can often encourage flexibility in the application of those procedures that exist. He can plan curriculum that may obviously indicate administrative changes. He may also encourage other teachers to consider administrative changes that benefit all students while helping slow learners. The teacher will be best prepared to undertake these and similar tasks only if he understands the over-all administrative structure and priorities in his own school and school system, and he must be aware of the existing arguments and research for and against specific administrative procedures as applied to slow learners. The teacher does not administer, but he can be a vital force in determining over-all administrative policy.

The most pressing and, as yet, unresolved question facing the teacher of slow learners is: "What is the best way to group the slow learner for instruction?" This question occurs because, even when he is very young, the slow child's learning characteristics tax the school's standard administrative and curriculum structure and suggest the formation of some special alternatives to the regular program. As the slow student grows older, his learning problems are often compounded by the appearance of disruptive or deviant behavior. Such behavior tends to reinforce the suggestion that the slow learner be educated with those of his own intellectual level. Implementations of this suggestion are based on local needs and experience rather than on solutions that have been developed through research methods and demonstration programs. Accordingly, the resulting groups of slow learners are quite varied.

Grouping methods frequently adopted by individual school systems are:

1. Academic achievement grouping
2. Social development grouping
3. Special class grouping
4. Homogeneous grouping

These grouping types are not self-inclusive and are frequently seen in combination; also, each type suggests only a general approach. There are many specific meanings given to each type as it is applied by individual school systems.

Academic Achievement Grouping. This method places all students in the same class and presents them with the same learning material. When a student shows he has mastered the academic information required of his present grade, he is moved to the next grade. If the student learns quickly, he may skip a grade. If the student learns slowly, he will "stay back." Academic achievement grouping appears to be quite incompatible with slow learning. It denies the child's learning problems and relegates him to a low status position. The only challenge that the teacher may offer the slow learner is one that leads to failure. Although rigid academic achievement grouping is rarely seen in modern elementary schools, it is still prevalent in the high schools, particularly in communities where most graduates enter college. Technically, all students in these communities are not expected to meet the same standards; but, since they offer only a college-preparatory sequence, it is impossible for such schools to prepare the non-college-bound student for life to the same degree that the college-bound student is prepared for higher education. As Conant [18] notes:

> Increased attention ought to be paid in both slums and suburbs to developing meaningful courses for pupils with less than average abilities. To this end, consideration should be given by every school and community to the expansion of work study programs for slow students. . . .

Social Development Grouping. This method of grouping attempts to remove all academic pressure from the student with an underlying philosophy that the school is primarily an instrument of personal social growth and that academic achievement, while important to this growth, cannot be allowed to dominate it. The social development approach allows a student to move through school with his peers on the basis of his general social adjustment and personal maturity. The advantages to slow learners of removing academic pressure are obvious, although complete removal may result in minimal academic achievement. The social development approach also has the advantage of encouraging instructional emphasis on those social skills that are so necessary to adult adjustment. These advantages can be realized, however, only if the concept is implemented with small classes, well-trained teachers, and adequate support from psychological, remedial, and curriculum enrichment resources.

The main limitation of this grouping plan is that the teacher must individualize instruction for pupils whose range of abilities widens considerably with age. For this reason, social development grouping or its parallel designation, social promotion, begins to lose its effectiveness after grade four, and it becomes almost impossible to continue in the junior and senior high schools.

Special Class Grouping. Under this type of grouping, slow learners are removed from the main stream of education and placed in a setting that, through the use of special teachers, curriculum, and materials, allows close control of the child's learning environment. The special class isolates the child from the ridicule and failure he faces when competing with normal peers. By reducing class size and concentrating on a specific learning problem, the special class gives the teacher more freedom to plan a specialized educational program.

The disadvantages of special classes, however, cannot be waved away. Self-containment tends to stigmatize students and teachers and may also alienate parents. The rather high per pupil cost of the special class program is an additional disadvantage as is the fact that there is a scarcity of the highly trained personnel so necessary to the success of such classes. Also, present curriculum plans do not ensure capitalization of the best features of special class grouping. A very practical consideration in arguing against the establishment of special classes is the sheer size of the slow learning problem. The incidence rates cited earlier indicate that if special classes were to be provided for all slow learners, their occupants would constitute 15 to 20 per cent of the total school population. The mentally retarded, who constitute only 2 to 3 per cent of the school population, have been provided for in self-contained groups for many years, and special classes are mandated by law in a number of states. Yet, Mackie [60] reports that only one-third of the mentally retarded have their needs met through special class placement. The implication for slow learning is obvious.

In view of their disadvantages, it would appear that relatively few self-contained classes would be established. This conclusion is supported by the undocumented statements of Abraham [2] and Johnson [48]. One study that supports self-contained classroom placement is reported by Reid [70]. Her group ranged in I.Q. from 67 to 79 as measured, in part, by group tests and, in part, by individual tests. No measure of central tendency was given. In the five-year study period, the special class students remained in school longer, had a lower reported delinquency rate, and participated in more school activities than similar students who remained in regular classes. This study is reminiscent of many similar studies designed to test the relative merits of special class placement for the mentally retarded. In a review of these studies, Kirk [53] indicates that although more than a dozen attempts have been made to compare the effectiveness of special versus regular classes, results are inconclusive and cannot be used to form reliable generalizations. He places specific blame for this condition on the difficulties inherent in conducting such studies and on the lack of suitable measuring instruments.

Homogeneous Grouping. This method places together all students having similar ability levels and academic achievements. Homogeneous grouping seems to be more democratic than the special class because it does not emphasize an individual's uniqueness. It allows more flexible movement of teachers and students and can be varied in several ways. For example, groups may be composed of a mixture of normal and slower students and normal and brighter students. Homogeneous grouping is the most popular plan adopted by secondary schools and has many adherents at the upper elementary level as well. Arguments against homogeneous grouping stress the fact that, particularly in the early school years, such grouping may unnecessarily predetermine a child's future on the basis of some rather inadequate identification procedures. Homogeneous grouping also tends to concentrate behavior problems and is often a relatively simple administrative solution that serves to avoid such difficult questions as: "How can effective, interesting curriculum content be developed for all children?" and "How can a school philosophy be developed that avoids classifying the slow learner as an instructional burden who is best removed from the regular classroom?" West [87] discusses these and other questions in his report on a study conducted in a Dade County, Florida, elementary school. He reports that slow learners who were grouped homogeneously achieved greater academic success but developed noticeable negative personal and social attitudes. The teachers who participated indicated that they favored special grouping but preferred not to teach such classes.

Arguments against homogeneous grouping tend to be muffled in the secondary schools. Subject matter departmentalization creates a precedent for grouping that makes its adoption appear quite logical. Since the label "slow learning" is considered to be fairly accurate by the time a child reaches the secondary school level, there is less concern over premature grouping and parental furor. Varney [84] comments:

> In reality, the question to be faced is not whether there will be separation, but rather the kind and degree of separation that should exist, since some degree of separation is to be found in nearly all secondary schools.

Utley [83] suggests that careful personal guidance may help the older slow learner understand his learning problem and thus soften the adverse personal reaction that he may experience upon being removed from the college-bound stream. One grouping problem that persists even with the most adequate supporting services is that administrative changes often are not accompanied by comparable curriculum revisions. Until a proper emphasis is placed on what the student learns, the locus of his learning is somewhat unimportant.

A review of commonly implemented grouping procedures suggests that heterogeneous grouping is the first choice of elementary schools. Junior and senior high schools favor homogeneously grouped classes, ability tracks, or similar arrangements that tend to isolate learners according to their intellectual or academic performance level. There is no research evidence at any grade level that gives conclusive support to any one type of grouping. There is some indication that homogeneous groups frequently are formed to relieve administrative pressures or to control poor behavers who appear in heterogeneous groups that are inadequately supported or poorly taught. The teacher must remember that whatever his procedural preferences, grouping, in itself, is not the total solution to the problems of slow learning. Grouping should be considered as but one interrelated element of a comprehensive educational structure. The administrative framework of this structure will include attention to teacher selection, curriculum development, grading procedures, promotion standards, and related factors.

Featherstone [97] has indicated:

> There is much to be said both for and against separate grouping, but the significance of what might be said varies from school to school. . . . At least this much can be said. Mere separation without far-reaching reconstruction of the curriculum will accomplish little for the slow pupils. . . . On the other hand, leaving slow learners in mixed groups will not ease their burdens either or prevent experiences of inadequacy, feelings of in-

feriority, and the development of possible antisocial attitudes, unless the program in the mixed groups is very flexible and adaptable to a wide range of needs and abilities. . . . In the final analysis each school must size up its own situation.

No matter what procedure the teacher prefers, it should be remembered that grouping decisions cannot be applied indiscriminately to groups of children. Grouping is designed essentially to meet individual instructional problems. Some slow learners will profit most from placement with other slow learners. Some will learn best when educated within a regular classroom. Others will gain most from moving between these alternatives as their tolerances permit. Ideally, a school system should provide several flexible grouping arrangements. Grouping policy is usually couched in terms that do not offer the slow student a choice suited to his personal learning problems. He is expected to meet standards established by educational consensus even though he may be the exception that proves the rule.

SELECTION PROCEDURES

Once a grouping policy is adopted, careful selection procedures must be developed to ensure that student characteristics will harmonize with the policy's specific features. Selection procedures have received little attention since most teachers and administrators are satisfied with the initial process of identification and are content to plan programs around a general label. Usually, slow learners are massed for programs rather than selected for them. Consequently, the teacher finds it difficult to identify common learning problems, to plan for a workable range of academic levels, or to formulate a cohesive approach to class discipline. The establishment and successful operation of any program for slow learners, heterogeneous or homogeneous, depends upon the specification of definite goals and the selection of students who can be expected to achieve those goals. For example, if a school establishes a special remedial class designed to return slow learners to the regular course of study, priority should be given to underachieving culturally deprived or minimally brain damaged slow learners who appear to be of average intelligence. Similarly, when a school plans a school work-study program for slow learners, it should select students who show limited academic potential, but who also have expressed interest in vocational exploration and who give evidence of the general social and emotional maturity that is required by the structure of the work-study program. As a final example, the teacher who plans to group slow learners within his class should select them only after gaining a thorough knowledge of their learning problems and assessing honestly the specific assistance he is capable of offering each child. Whatever the school's purposes in educating slow learners, these purposes cannot be met without a careful selection of students. Well-developed selection procedures are useful in highlighting weaknesses in the school's total plan of services.

CLASS SIZE

The research on class size appears to indicate that there is no optimum size nor an ideal ratio between teachers and students, although small classes do make it easier to effect attitude and behavior changes. Discipline problems do appear to grow as classes grow larger, although learning rate seems to be affected by many factors other than class size. The teacher seems to be the crucial element in determining class size as his instructional approach and behavior tolerance level are the factors that will determine how many or how few students he can handle [Holland and Galfo, 46].

It is apparent that class size must be considered in at least two dimensions. First, the size of the heterogeneous class in which slow learners are grouped with normal and bright students; and, second, the size of the homogeneous class in which slow learners are grouped together.

In a heterogeneous group where the teacher is acquainted with slow learning and is skilled in individualizing instruction, it would appear that there is no quarrel with the twenty-five-member class generally recommended for modern public schools. This number, however, is flexible and should be decided on after an analysis of the general behavioral atmosphere of the classroom—not merely through a count of the number of slow learners present. Normal and bright students may also make unusual demands on the teacher. Some heterogeneous classes function well with thirty pupils or more; others generate persistent problems even when staffed by a superior teacher with responsibility for fifteen pupils or less.

Homogeneous group size must also be kept flexible although these classes are generally smaller than their heterogeneous counterparts. The size reduction is consistent with the research literature. Available study data indicate that when grouping is based on problem behavior there are few students who can release the teacher for individualized instruction by working on their own or by helping the less able. Also, if pupils selected for homogeneous grouping have social and behavioral characteristics that the school hopes to change, this change will be effected more readily in a small group.

In homogeneous or heterogeneous groups, the final decision on class size should be postponed until an analysis is available of how well each student attains realistic educational goals through teacher-group interaction.

INTEGRATION

The slow learner often becomes a social isolate despite implementation of the best-planned grouping practices. It is the responsibility of the school and the teacher to afford the slow learner the same treatment as that given all other children except where such treatment will exacerbate his learning problem. Too often the slow learner is excluded from school activities only because teachers or administrators have a feeling that "he wouldn't fit." In such cases, it is the school's responsibility to make adjustments so the slow learner's "fit" is accomplished. The special subject areas, social activities, athletics, and other school programs should be available to the slow student and his involvement in them should be encouraged. The introduction of study units related to these and other school activities will help ensure the slow learner's success in activities with other students. Whenever the problem of integrating the slow learner occurs, it is important to ask the following questions in sequence:

Why is the slow learner excluded?
On what basis should he be included?
How is this inclusion to be accomplished?

COMMUNICATION

Bad news travels rapidly, and the slow learner is generally known to almost everyone in the school because he has been identified as a problem. His strength and the ways in which the entire school may help him are less well known. The teacher who intends to build an adequate program must learn how to impart information to teachers and students that will assist in building positive attitudes toward slow learners. The information to be disseminated must be chosen carefully. It must neither be too technical nor too personal. Before any information is distributed, the teacher should assess the selected audience's readiness to accept and profit from such information.

REMEDIAL SERVICES

Administrative provisions for slow learning are incomplete without attention to various remedial services. Remedial reading will assist the large number of slow learners who have remedial as well as developmental reading problems. Speech correctionists may help slow learners overcome basic speech difficulties that retard their communication. Social-service workers can be employed to help the slow child's family understand his slowness and to assist them in overcoming home problems that may create slowness. Psychological services are essential for a primary diagnosis, for reassessing the child's intellectual function, and for interpreting behavior to teachers, administrators, and parents. Adequate medical and dental services are necessary to the diagnosis and treatment of the slow learner's health problems. A librarian and an instructional materials specialist will provide enrichment. Community agencies should also be included in the complete remedial plan for slow learners; recreation and welfare services are particularly useful in supplementing the work of the school. It is the teacher's responsibility to refer the slow student to all available remedial services and continually to assess his ability to profit from them.

GUIDANCE

Special guidance programs for slow learners are infrequently cited either because of a lack of interest or, hopefully, because the slow learner may be best served through the school's standard guidance procedures. The guidance topics discussed with slow learners most often relate to the reduction of problem behavior and the continuation of remedial procedures introduced in the school's instructional phase. Specific concerns center on the child's feelings of alienation from the society of the school, his search for self-identity and self-confidence in a world where high value is placed on attributes he does not possess, the family problems related to academic slowness, and the development of socially acceptable ways of handling and expressing the feelings that his many problems create.

The most difficult guidance task is establishing insights in a child who, by definition, has limited ability to handle the abstractions necessary for the development of such insights. Despite his limited reasoning powers, the slow learner can profit from individual counseling if it is planned to meet his needs. A report by Sorenson [75] indicates that short-term counseling is not especially effective but that a long-range counseling program can be helpful if it includes the teacher and the parent.

There does not appear to be any one counseling approach best suited to the intellectual level of slow learners, although it does appear that the possibility of achieving favorable results will be improved if the technique chosen is based on the child's behavior. In a summary of a series of studies on the effectiveness of specific counseling approaches with the retarded, Beier [10] notes:

> There is some indication that the more directive and structured psychotherapeutic approaches are more effective with the aggressively acting-out, sociopathic, and delinquent varieties of retardates, and the more non-directive techniques with the withdrawn, shy, and anxious types.

Group counseling appears to be an attractive technique for use with slow learners. It is economical in terms of time, money, and professional manpower because it allows the counselor to reach fairly large groups, and it permits the slow learner to achieve the feeling of belonging to a group. Lodato and Sokoloff [58] report on a group counseling project with slow learners in which they used a persuasive approach and consistently set certain definite limits on the amount of disruptive or aggressive behavior permitted. Their results are encouraging although the study suffers from the methodological weaknesses seen in most reports of group counseling experiments. These weaknesses make it difficult to draw any definite conclusions concerning the over-all effectiveness of group counseling.

If a group counseling program for slow learners is to be established, the following cautions should be observed:

1. The goals of the group counseling program must be limited in keeping with the counseling skills and resources available.
2. The goals should be designed to change behavior and not to improve reading skill or effect similar changes that are better accomplished by other means.
3. The expected results should be testable in well-defined terms that are established before the program is instituted.
4. The program should be part of a total instructional approach whose other segments supplement and support group counseling goals.

Because guidance is a basic part of any program for the slow learner, the teacher should have training in basic guidance techniques and be sensitized to the subtleties of referral. Group and individual guidance with the slow learner require more time than the school usually allots to this function. Accordingly, guidance must be planned as a definite part of the daily schedule so that it is not accomplished on a "catch as catch can" basis. In addition to benefiting from the teacher's efforts at guidance, slow learners would appear to profit from the increasing provision of formal guidance services in the elementary grades and the stress placed on guidance as a tool to reduce secondary school dropouts.

RECORD KEEPING

Much of the existent confusion about slow learning would be eliminated if all teachers kept more complete records of personality and behavior. The problem behaver in junior high school has developed his behavior pattern slowly over the years in reaction to a great number of situations presented by the school. Unfortunately, it is usually only the sum of these reactions that is available. If records were more complete and based on well-structured observation techniques, it would be possible to treat behavioral causes more often, rather than defend against behavioral symptoms. While this is a plea for better record keeping in general, there are several specific points that are important if adequate records for slow learners are to be developed.

The records usually kept by schools stress academic adjustment since a history of such adjustment is vital to decisions concerning future educational placement. Good academic records are equally important for the slow learner and should reflect the internal elements and incidental steps in his academic progress. Teaching procedures or methods that appear to be most effective should be noted. Records should indicate what subject matter appeared to interest the child, as well as those studies that seemed to frustrate him. Such record keeping will inform future teachers about methods tried and subject material covered, thus offering a basis for analyzing the extent of the child's past learning opportunities and for evaluating the relative success of various teaching approaches. This type of record keeping is time consuming, but it can be systematized by studying each student in sequence and using a checklist that provides space to record the activity attempted, the method used, and the reaction seen. Such a checklist should be developed by the school as a whole to ensure consistency in reporting.

Record keeping for the slow learner will place more than usual emphasis on social adjustment and on those aspects of behavior that relate closely to future vocational success. It will be helpful to know how the slow learner makes friends and with whom he chooses to associate, or rather, by whom he is accepted. What are his work habits? What special skills or interests does he have that might be vocationally useful? What is his level of frustration? What behavioral approaches work best with him when he is depressed, aggressive, argumentive, or when he exhibits other forms of behavior which the teacher feels should be changed? What are the educational and vocational resources of his home and local community? In what ways does he react to authority? How concrete must directions be before he can follow them without further assistance? How persistent is the student in following through on academic tasks? Non-academic tasks? Information that answers these and similar questions should be available in the slow learner's record. Record keeping should include positive information as well as nuggets of the negative kind so often associated with slow learning. Positive information need not be trivial or invented. It will appear naturally and regularly if the observer is truly objective and has learned how to recognize it.

MARKING

"Mark liberally" is somewhat typical of advice given to teachers when they ask the question, "How do I mark the slow learner?" Such advice reflects the confusion that exists concerning basic reasons why marks are given. It also appears to indicate the educator's understandable unwillingness to face the problems inherent in having the slow learner recognize failure.

Marks are intended to indicate the relationship between actual achievement and expected achievement. Theoretically, marks are a system of shorthand that indicates an individual's relative competency in what he has been taught. If marks were used simply to show a student where he stands in relation to what he should know, there would be no question about using marks with slow learners. However, in reality marks are not used primarily as a shorthand that provides for individual comparison. Marks generally are considered to be an indication of how well a person compares with other persons or groups. When used for general comparison, marks become the medium through which the slow learner measures his failure and, consequently, his worth in the world of the school. Marks tend to threaten the slow learner's self-concept and may arouse emotional defenses that serve as impediments to learning.

In addition to their function as a measuring stick, marks are also an important part of the school's reward system. High marks are felt to result in increased learning motivation while poor marks are seen as decreasing such motivation. Consequently, when the teacher encounters slow learners he may feel that he can reduce feelings of failure and avoid a drop in motivation by deciding to "grade liberally." Yet, the slow learner expects to be marked, knows how to use this information in comparing himself with others, and is quite aware of the effort he has expended. He and his fellow students soon learn the emptiness of unearned rewards.

The solution to the marking dilemma lies in re-thinking what marks can mean to the slow learner. He can learn to accept failure in his comparison with others if he knows success in reaching goals that he has been involved in establishing. He can learn to live with his marks if they are interpreted as a means for evaluating the individual's growth and as a measure of competence in the level of subject matter his ability permits him to master. The slow learner can learn that a person makes marks: marks do not make the person. The teacher should "plan instruction liberally" but should not "grade liberally."

REPORTING

School reports are used to record and disseminate information about a student's marks and school behavior, and other aspects of his performance that are necessary to evaluate present educational progress and formulate future life goals. Reporting procedures should be a vehicle for transporting information, not a stricture that determines how such information will be collected and evaluated. Teachers interested in slow students are particularly vexed with reporting procedures as these procedures encourage comparison between students who are unequal intellectually and thus have no common academic goal.

One attempt to eliminate the comparison problem has been to use a general reporting system. The substitution of two general symbols (S or U, P or F) for a set of specifically progressive symbols (A, B, C, D, etc.) is a device commonly used in the primary grades. The addition to this system of I (improving) is a refinement of particular usefulness to slow learners as it indicates that, although their work does not meet grade standards, it is equal to the effort expended. The system does not keep students from comparing progress, and the consistent passing marks may lead parent and child to adopt a false sense of academic security. Also, there is no provision for ranking groups in terms of individual performance and for establishing the academic cut-off points stipulated in the entrance requirements of certain schools or colleges.

The written report details the child's progress in specific subject matter skills and also gives an indication of his social and emotional development. It is another fairly popular attempt to reduce the harmful effect of comparisons while building aspiration levels. Written reports sometimes frustrate the teacher because he may have very little academic progress to report or has difficulty in finding enough other information of a "positive" nature. Also, some teachers do not express themselves well enough to be appreciated by parents of high socioeconomic status while others express themselves too well to be understood by parents from deprived areas. Written reports are time consuming, and their lack of conciseness often violates the prime rule that reports should convey approximately the same ideas to all who read them.

Some school systems report performance on checklists. This reporting format allows the teacher a variety of responses while reducing the amount of time required and standardizing the reporting language. The checklist, however, often becomes an elaborated report card on which subject comments are substituted for letter grading. The checklist, although well intended, suffers from the same basic problems as does its model.

These are but a few of the basic reporting systems that may be considered. Their merits and faults will be judged within the philosophical framework of each school system, administrator, and teacher. Accordingly, it is impossible to reach a general conclusion as to which system is the best.

If the teacher is free to do so, he may wish to consider the alternative of giving slow learners two sets of marks [Johnson, 48]. One set would reflect the student's progress in relation to his ability; the second set would report how well he achieves when compared to non-slow leaners. This system would require a thorough introductory procedure and constant re-evaluation so that parents would be able to accept the differences between the grades given and be able to apply the student's self-comparison to academic or vocational plans.

PROMOTION AND GRADUATION

The grouping procedures used in individual school systems will determine the promotion and graduation guidelines followed for the slow child. No matter what policies are formulated, they should be consistent with the following principles:

1. Promotion and graduation should represent positive rewards for reaching an established level of academic competence. The level should be varied according to differing abilities. Denial of these rewards should not be used to punish a student for being unable to achieve goals that are beyond his ability.
2. Retention in a grade is justified only if the school expends the extra effort necessary to make the repeated year a new learning

experience and only if it appears that the child has the ability and the motivation to profit from this experience.

3. The slow learner has been different all through school. When he leaves school, however, his obvious differences will disappear. The graduation ceremony is an appropriate time to remember this fact.
4. The school should involve the slow learner in decisions concerning promotion and graduation. This involvement may be accomplished by carefully defining to the student the steps to promotion and graduation and identifying for him the point at which each of these steps is reached.

RESEARCH

One of the few constants in the field of slow learning is the complaint concerning the dearth of carefully designed and scientifically controlled research. The research results that are available are frequently inconclusive because subjects are poorly defined, defined in widely different terms, or not defined at all. Yet, much of the confusion and lack of progress in the field can be traced directly to the fact that very little good research exists.

A basic question that must be approached through research is: "Who are the slow learners?" A workable definition of slow learning cannot be developed until it is known precisely what types of pupils presently are identified as slow learners and whether or not the criteria used for identification are consistent from kindergarten through high school. Knowledge is required about the kinds of grouping plans used and the merits of each as evaluated by carefully controlled research. A study must be made concerning the transferabality to slow learning of research information gathered on bright, normal, and retarded children. The curriculum area offers a rather endless number of research opportunities as does the question: "Who should teach the slow learner?"

If the field of slow learning is to move from a base of conjecture to one of fact, a basic research emphasis must be incorporated into each school's program, and the teacher must consider himself the primary agent for identifying research problems and applying research results.

THE TEACHER

The teacher is the key in translating a concern for slow learning into a program of effective action. Teachers who work with slow learners should be able to provide effective instruction for children and to influence positively the entire school's attitude toward slow learning. The teacher must be intelligent and perceptive in order to match behavioral clues to instructional resources. He must not forget that slow students may be unable to follow the abstractions that accompany the teacher's brightness. He must be adaptive and know how to discover and apply new teaching ideas. Yet, he must not adjust so rapidly that students are unable to follow his adaptations. Patience is essential if the child is to have the time and opportunity to express himself; but the child must also have a measure of instructional challenge born of intellectual impatience. The teacher should know how to minimize unnecessary failure. He must also know how to teach the child what failure means and how it may provide positive learnings. The teacher should exercise his imagination concerning program goals but must always temper his dreams with the reality of the child's background and the attitudes of school and society.

The successful teacher of slow learners is a committed teacher. He has chosen a slow group as his initial assignment or has remained teaching them after his seniority would allow him to accept another assignment. There is no evidence to indicate which of many possible motives are the source of this commitment. However, the motives that usually result in failure are fairly well known. A teacher will not find success with slow learners if he thinks that the group's diminished brainpower will demand less of his intelligence; if he has experienced failure or uneasiness in other assignments; if he is attracted only by the extra money sometimes paid; or if he has a need to dominate a group. Teachers should have the opportunity to volunteer for teaching a slow group instead of being assigned because they are the newest or poorest teachers—this practice may be more frequent than is admitted.

Experience with normal children appears to be useful in teaching the slow child as it gives the teacher a frame of reference for judging academic and social growth. Unfortunately, some teachers are unable to rise above their past experience, and they establish goals and remedial procedures designed to help the child meet the teacher's normal expectations. Some administrators recommend that teachers experienced and certified in mental retardation be assigned to schools or classes where slow learners predominate. However, such teachers, if they can be found, may not expect enough of the child and may formulate goals that result in removing the slow learner from the educational mainstream.

Whether it be quiet or noisy, aggressiveness is an essential characteristic for teachers of slow learners. A willingness to be self-starting and to follow through is necessary in a program that is often seen as a convenient depository for failing students. Aggressiveness in the form of persistence is also required if the student is to be motivated to learn. The ability to gain cooperation and active assistance from the rest of the school is another task that will require persistent aggressiveness.

The teacher of slow learners should have strong intellectual curiosity and be willing to experiment. He must be sensitive to the slow child's needs and be able to place these needs ahead of those usually given priority by the school. Such teaching is based on a philosophy born of experiment and on a manner derived from observation. Methodology and technique are the servants of need, not its predetermined master.

The teacher of slow learners is also responsible for determining those over-all school changes that may assist him in his instructional tasks. The process begins with an examination of the programs and materials used with normal children. What is absurd for the normal child, and schools do perpetuate a few absurdities, will usually be even more inappropriate for slow learners. Teachers are generally apprehensive about suggesting changes since they are fearful that their superiors will feel threatened. Some easily threatened supervisors and administrators do exist, but most see good innovation as an asset. Teachers who can frame an idea for change in a nonthreatening way—and this process can be learned—will often improve instruction.

Hopefully, the attributes discussed will not be restricted to those teachers who are sought for homogeneous groups of slow learners. With few exceptions, every teacher is a teacher of the slow learner and must have the interest, the skills, and the attitudes to program effectively for him. Teachers at all levels need to be introduced to the problems of slow learning as part of their training. Such exposure is particularly essential for junior and senior high school teachers as their education is so heavily content oriented. A general survey course on slow learning may be very useful to all teachers. It is particularly necessary for teachers of homogeneous groups. Such a course will be most effective if presented to teachers who have teaching experience against which to weigh the concepts presented. The in-service program is probably the most efficient way to reach the many teachers who have little or no background in slow learning. Such programs, even when augmented with a survey course, are not enough preparation for teachers of homogeneous groups or special programs. These teachers should receive the benefit of a comprehensive program designed to give them skills in guidance, counseling, vocational orientation, educational materials' construction and presentation, classroom observation and evaluation, and the ability to understand and provide for the problems that characterize the many subgroups that comprise the constellation of slow learning. A course of study designed specifically to prepare specialists in slow learning does not, as yet, appear to exist, and it may be counted as another of the relatively unexplored aspects of the field.

SUMMARY

Some of the areas that must be considered by teachers when they plan the administrative aspects of programming are:

1. Grouping
2. Selection Procedures
3. Class Size
4. Integration
5. Communication
6. Remedial Services
7. Guidance
8. Record Keeping
9. Marking
10. Reporting
11. Promotion and Graduation
12. Research
13. Teacher Competencies

There is very little research to support the adoption of any fixed administrative guidelines in any of the areas considered. Rather, decisions must be made at the local level after weighing the type or types of slow learners enrolled, the level at which these learners are accepted by the school, the specific adaptability of the school itself, and the willingness of the school to expend the effort and money required by certain choices. Ideally, administrative provisions for the slow learner will not be determined on an either-or basis but will provide the flexibility necessary to meet individual needs.

CHAPTER V

Curriculum

The most carefully formulated administrative approaches to slow learning will be effective only if they are accompanied by corresponding care in instructional planning. Despite their importance, curriculum plans that effectively meet the slow learner's needs are not prevalent. Apparently, necessary curriculum revisions are frustrated by an educational tradition that insists that the child be fitted to the curriculum rather than having the curriculum fit the child: "We are more interested in what children study than in what study does to children" [Melby, 131]. "Public schooling may be less a positive preparation for success in the world of work than a screening device for the working world" [Robinson, 136]. Often, the curriculum is seen as an essential guide that is sent for, taught from, and revised as ritual demands. In fact, many teachers and others concerned with the schools take the curriculum for granted, almost as they would a natural phenomena, and consider it to be a document that has gained credence and authority through the test of time, or through the imprimatur of their state department of education. Such attitudes lead to curriculum consumption, rather than to creative curriculum development. Rarely is the curriculum seen as an experimental statement of direction keyed to the careful observation of individual needs.

Every teacher who works with slow learners must seek active involvement in curriculum development. This involvement may be limited to revising mathematics materials to meet more effectively the needs of a single child, or it may be as extensive as membership on a committee to plan a new system-wide curriculum for slow students. At whatever level the teacher becomes associated with curriculum improvement, he must remember that curriculum begins with the child and is built to meet the child's needs. To assist the teacher in improving his curriculum-building skills, this chapter will consider curriculum sources, choices, and other constants that underlie curriculum construction; Chapter VII will discuss the specific instructional adaptations that may form part of a curriculum for slow learners.

CURRICULUM DEFINITION

The teacher who searches for the guidance of a curriculum definition will find many voices chanting many themes. Addressing itself to a national audience, the N.E.A. Research Division [132] offered the following definition: "The curriculum for the slow learner is similar to that for the normal pupil but is adapted to the nature of his learning process." Shawn [141] writing for a statewide audience indicates:

> The needs of this group of learners can be met best by revising curriculum and presenting it in terms of the limited academic achievement levels and, in some cases, the potentiality of these children.

Featherstone [126] states that curriculum goals must be immediate and tangible, and that curriculum activities must be concrete. Strom [78] notes that:

> Determination of course offerings could, in part, be established on the basis of: (1) what is known about why these pupils reject school; (2) the unique characteristics of these pupils; and (3) the occupational outlook for the future.

These and similar statements are in keeping with the uncertainty surrounding the definition of slow learning; they suggest that curriculum development has not yet reached the stage of being a carefully organized process based on deeply held philosophical convictions founded in empirical and research evidence. At present, the teacher can conclude that there exists no single acceptable definition of an adequate curriculum for slow learners. Accordingly, the teacher's working definition must reflect the needs of his local community and its specific definition of slow learning.

CURRICULUM SOURCES

The sources from which the slow learner's curriculum is derived are the same as those that influence curriculum development for all children. These sources include:

1. The traditions of education and society
2. A study of the nature of the learner
3. A study of the child's present and predicted environment

4. Curriculum guides used in the schools
5. Follow-up studies
6. Teacher opinion

While traces of each of these sources can be found to varying degrees in almost every curriculum, it is the usual practice to have only one of them noticeably dominant. Such dominance is determined by the community's character and the way this character influences the schools. In individual school systems, the source chosen to give major curriculum direction to the normal child often determines the extent and direction of curriculum development for slow learners.

CURRICULUM CHOICES

Slow Track Curriculum. The majority of schools determine their curriculum focus on the basis of the traditions of education and society. Consequently, the curriculum choice most commonly found for slow learners is the slow track curriculum. The slow track approach usually called "the watered down curriculum" by its detractors, is based on the assumption that slow learners will gain the greatest benefit from approximately the same learning material that is given to the normal child. It is assumed further that this material can be learned if a sympathetic teacher presents it slowly, repetitively, and in an interesting manner. The essential elements of the slow track curriculum are the provision of the necessary time and motivation for learning. The plan is a response to the concern for individual differences, but it has neither the inherent philosophy nor structure to provide for the psychosocial problems that these differences tend to produce.

The slow track approach is frequently proposed as a hedge against the recognized inadequacy of present diagnostic measures. Slowing the regular curriculum rather than changing its basic structure allows the wrongly diagnosed child who begins to show academic improvement to be easily transferred to the regular track. The slow track curriculum usually does not appear as a separate curriculum document, although some systems do publish a booklet of guidelines designed to help the teacher recognize and meet the psychological characteristics and learning needs of the slower child. Schools that use the slow track approach frequently appoint committees to rewrite traditional materials, to evaluate novel approaches to the presentation of standard content, and to select texts or other commercial materials that present basic material on several different reading or comprehension levels.

The slow track curriculum usually appears in its complete form in the primary and intermediate grades. Here, the problems of slow learning are still considered primarily to be instructional, and their solution is sought through greater attention on the part of the teacher and more practice on the part of the student. Slow tracking, as a total approach, would appear to be most appropriate in grades 1, 2, 3, and possibly 4, since these grades contain the basic academic content of what is commonly considered to be an education. If the child is diverted from the basics before he has had an opportunity to master them, there is concern that the product of any following curriculum can only be disappointing. Perhaps much of the later fumbling for curriculum could be avoided if the early school years were devoted to teaching fundamental academic skills on the basis of a careful analysis of the child's learning process and of the gaps in his essential learning experiences.

When employed in secondary schools, the slow track curriculum often presents the slow student with learning experiences only in those subjects that appear appropriate to his intellectual level. The content may simply be slowed, or it may be closely tied to a remedial approach. In the secondary schools, the slow track curriculum usually consists of a series of isolated subject adaptations that do not result in comprehensive curriculum planning. This situation arises from the departmentalized nature of the secondary school, which makes it difficult to cross-reference curriculum content. It is also the result of the training that secondary school teachers have had which makes it much easier for them to adapt their subject content rather than to integrate it into an over-all curriculum design. The apparent inability to effect a successful transfer of the slow track curriculum from elementary to secondary schools has caused many educators to decry the programs for slow learners at the secondary level and, by implication, to condemn elementary school slow track curriculum as well. This condemnation has not produced any significant experimentation in curriculum improvement for slow learners in the primary and intermediate grades, but it has placed an onus on any discussion of slow tracking in general. There is urgent need to measure the advantages and disadvantages of a complete slow track curriculum before such curriculum is condemned.

Life-centered Approach. School systems that base their curriculum on a study of the child's environment usually develop a curriculum design that is life-oriented rather than subject-oriented. This design is not unique to programs for slow learners, but it appears to have advantages that make it especially suited for use with them. The life-centered approach appeals to slow learners because its novelty overcomes the aura of failure associated with the traditional approaches they have known. Since a large proportion of slow learners live in impoverished homes or deprived environments, the life-oriented curriculum should be more efficient because it encourages the child to begin learning at his own experience level. This approach, through its emphasis on core learnings and activity units, allows the teacher many opportunities to move from the concrete to the abstract. This emphasis also allows the child to become more involved in his education. Since this approach does not consider education primarily as preparation for college, it provides more post-school choices for the slow learner.

Literature that discusses the life-centered approach with slow learners contains few references to the use of this approach in the primary and elementary grades. However, it appears that the design is appropriate after slow learners have achieved at least minimal academic competence and before they discover that their skills, though credible, are inadequate to meet the increasing demands of the regular curriculum. The absence of specific subject matter demands appears to make the life-centered curriculum quite transferable to the junior and senior high school. When this curriculum is used in secondary schools, blocks of time, encompassing several class periods are often set aside so that correlation of academic subject matter may be effected. The slow learners meet as a group for these sessions, but they learn with regular students in other activities, usually those in special subject areas such as art or physical education. When the slow students meet in their own groups, the academic content may be correlated under such headings as community-related academics [Seeley, 140] or the core academic period [Edwards, 124]. These programs emphasize social adjustment and the use of familiar materials in a relaxed learning atmosphere to promote the development of general vocational and life-adjustment skills [Herkner and Malone, 128; Pellman and Liddle, 133].

Critics of the life-centered approach contend that practical academics are worthless unless they are built on a strong foundation of developmental academics, a foundation that must be continually extended through the school years. It is said also that the life-centered approach requires a teacher who is sympathetic to its aims, is very skillful in assessing the needs of the class, and has the ability to integrate the diverse content of many subjects into a comprehensive presentation. Admittedly, such teachers are difficult to find. This approach can also be criticized because it lacks an obvious structure. Consequently, students may not equate it with the traditional concept of "education." This reaction may be quite common with the culturally deprived who tend to judge the future usefulness of their education by comparing it to the education given other students in the school.

The Prevocational Approach. The prevocational approach reflects an emphasis on information gained from a study of the learner, a study of society, and an analysis of follow-up reports on the adult adjustment of the slow child. This approach has been developed from the same philosophical base as the life-centered approach and is often used as an extension of it. The prevocational approach assumes that the slow learner will end his schooling upon or before graduation from high school, and that he should, therefore, receive intensive vocational preparation in his few remaining school years. The approach implies that the importance of work in our society will give purpose to the student's school experiences and reduce his need to drop out. The prevocational approach is especially popular and effective in school districts that have a tradition of vocational education. Its effectiveness is increased when an effort is made to have school students share in the vocational success of the program's graduates. For example, graduates may visit the school to talk to students, and the students may visit places where slower students have found jobs.

In theory, the prevocational approach may extend downward to include the clean-up period in kindergarten. Specific prevocational programs, however, are not usually implemented until junior high school, where a step-like progression is begun. This progression moves from general vocational exploration, to in-school work, to part-time work outside school, to full-time placement. The work progression and other program features vary considerably as this type of curriculum for slow learners is still considered experimental. The academics in the program are usually of the applied type. Some basic developmental and remedial instruction may be provided if, as often happens, the interest in work prompts a renewed interest in academics. The program culminates in a period of work-study, usually a year, when the student is employed for a specific period (one-half day, one week, one month) and attends school for an equal period of time.

The prevocational approach can be limiting, as its goals generally preclude education beyond high school. The program may motivate students to choose work over school before they are ready to work. It may also appear to offer an "easy" way out of school and thus encourage dropouts. The program may also result in the vocational underemployment of slow learners, as trial jobs may be limited to the accepted stereotypes of what slow learners can do rather than provide true testing grounds of the student's interests and abilities. Whatever its faults, the prevocational curriculum is, at present, creating considerable impact on the education of slow learners in junior and senior high schools.

The teacher of slow learners should be aware of the various curriculum approaches just discussed, and be at least acquainted with their many possible variations, modifications, and combinations. For example, Davis [122] describes a special-class high school program for students with intelligence quotients between 70 and 90 that places strong emphasis on remedial academics and has as its objective the return of the child to a regular class. Aside from becoming acqainted with the theory of curriculum development, the teacher will be interested in knowing the applications of this theory so that it will be possible for him to plan a suitable day-to-day program for his slower pupils. For, despite the variations in the over-all curriculum design, there are a number of curriculum constants that can be applied at each teaching level.

CURRICULUM DEVELOPMENT IN THE PRIMARY GRADES

Despite the fact that slow learning exists in its most undifferentiated state in the primary grades, the young slow learner manages better here than he will in any subsequent phase of his school career. This fortunate occurrence is more the result of the general structure of the primary curriculum than the existence of any conscious provisions for slow learners. The primary subject matter is limited to a fairly small number of content areas. Children are expected to grow more slowly as they develop fundamental skills. Competition is less because the spread of abilities is less. In addition, the primary teacher is quite aware of individual academic differences and is trained to plan curriculum experiences to meet them. While this situation benefits the slow child in the primary grades, its existence often delays systematic identification and remedial procedures until the child leaves the protective primary environment and enters the world of accelerated failure. It is recognized that many children, who eventually appear slow, could be saved that fate if the child were identified and provided for early in his school career. Bloom [91] concludes that it becomes more and more difficult to change many characteristics as the child grows older, and only unusual conditions are likely to stimulate change in later life.

Studies reported by Kirk [52] and Fouracre, Connor, and Goldberg [127] indicate that the mentally retarded, and by implication the slow learner, can actually achieve at a rate greater than that predicted for them, if they receive a program of special stimulation in the preschool or kindergarten years. Studies with the culturally deprived reported by Deutsch [123] also indicate the possibility of preventing slowness in school subjects by the institution of a carefully planned preschool program. The Head Start program has given graphic application of earlier research on improving the child's ability to learn through the use of preschool programs [Brittain, 118; Robinson, 137; Spacks, 143]. At present, however, not all children have the advantage of special preschool programs and the primary teacher must still be very aware of curriculum approaches that will assist his slow learners.

A prime curriculum concern for the young slow child is the development of perceptual motor skills. Drawing upon his experimental work with young children and earlier studies in brain injury, Kephart [111] describes a very complete series of activities designed to evaluate and develop the child's visual-motor skill potential. The child's development is considered in terms of such areas as the motor bases of achievement, the perceptual process, and space discrimination. Training activities matched to the author's "Perceptual Survey Rating Scale" are outlined in areas that include chalkboard training, sensory-motor training, and training form perception.

The teacher of young slow learners will also need to know the many activities for development of color perception, size discrimination, and other skills related to the concepts needed for reading and other academics. The curriculum developed by Connor and Talbot [120] and the teaching materials derived from this curriculum [Talbot, 148] will be of particular interest to teachers concerned with concept development.

A thorough program of language development is most crucial to the slow child's future school success, particularly for those children from deprived environments. The primary curriculum must include many opportunities for children to hear and, more importantly, to speak, write, or otherwise communicate their reactions to the very direct language-stimulating experiences with which they are provided.

Self-concept development must occupy an important place in the total teaching scheme. The child should be helped to know who he is, and the teacher must be very aware of the feelings he communicates to the child about his slowness. Parent feelings toward the child should be known, and it is certainly not too early to use any available psychological, social work, or guidance services to help the parents realize the role their feelings will play in the child's future development. The child needs to learn what realistic success is by being given activities in which such success can be earned.

The primary years are, of course, not devoted entirely to concept formation and social development. The concepts and social abilities must be related to the work of the school. The child will need specific academic readiness instruction for a longer than usual period, and his uneven development will require that readiness be continued in some areas at the same time that formal instruction is begun in others. Readiness must be closely related to a constant assessment of the child's school accomplishments and to an evaluation of the necessary experiences that are not being provided outside of school. Formal instruction, when started, will be based largely on the child's verbal language, will reflect his own experiences, and will have a strong activity orientation. Incidental learning is not incidental for slow learners. The printed names on objects in the room, time telling, and other learning that normal children seem to "pick up" cannot be left to chance observations. Incidental learnings should be included in the formal instructional program. A consistent method of word and number attack should be taught to the slow learner—but only when he has a very clear concept of what words and numbers mean in his environment and how he will use them. The slow learner must be helped to realize that instruction is largely sequential by being given materials that combine previously taught instructional elements and new learnings.

In short, the primary curriculum for the child who appears slow should be based on assessing the gaps in his experience, determining his level of performance, and constantly reassessing performance (with him)—thereby helping to prevent the habit of failure. The primary curriculum must be flexible and experimental, otherwise it will tend to perpetuate recognized slowness rather than to provide the child with significant learning choices. The primary curriculum may be described as a readiness curriculum, but it must provide much more than the regular readiness material and at a slower rate. It must increase the richness, variety, and concreteness of this material and must present it before, during, and after the traditionally defined readiness period.

CURRICULUM DEVELOPMENT IN THE INTERMEDIATE GRADES

Unfortunately, the curriculum of the intermediate grades often arrives too soon for the slow learner. He has not yet begun to consolidate his gains in the areas of basic subject content when he is asked to apply his knowledge to several new content areas. The culturally deprived slow learner is at a particular disadvantage in the intermediate school because of what Deutsch [123] refers to as the cumulative deficit hypothesis. This hypothesis is a research-supported statement in which the inappropriateness of present school programs for the culturally deprived appear to increase learning deficits rather than ameliorate them. This problem of cumulative deficits appears to be most acute for slow learners in the academic, slow track curriculum, but it can arise in any curriculum design. The teacher may overcome this problem, in part, by planning activities in social studies, science, and other content areas, that will provide the child with an opportunity to practice his reading and language skills while he learns new subject material. This approach will mean less reliance on reading subject texts for information, and it will require more attention to using the subject material as the topic of lessons in the basic academic skill areas. In effect, the teacher will be providing instruction in content areas that are closely tied to the child's level of reading and verbal understanding, rather than presenting material that cannot be effectively mastered because the child does not have the related skills to cope with its language abstractions.

The need to relate specific content to basic study skills and the need to make all learning more concrete may be fulfilled in the intermediate grades by introducing the unit method to the curriculum [Thorsell, 149]. As used with slow learners, the unit method refers to the practice of correlating all subject matter instruction to a central theme that is important to the group; this method is based on the concept that learning is more effective if it actively involves the learner and grows from interests stimulated by activities in his immediate experience. A unit might evolve naturally from the children's interest in their neighborhood. In a city school, located near the dock area, trucking terminals, or a rail yard, a unit on transportation might be a natural complement to everyday interests; map reading, time schedules, distance problems, and measures of size and volume might be some of the activities used to correlate arithmetic to the unit; safety in driving, operating a train, or loading cargo might be included as a topic in health. Communications activities would include the use of the telephone book to find addresses, reading advertisements, reading booklets and pamphlets supplied by transportation companies, and reading shipping notices in the newspaper. Activities in other subjects would suggest themselves as the unit progressed. As this example indicates, the unit is one way of meeting the slow student's need in a heterogeneous group: unit activities simplify the problem of individualizing instruction through providing many experiences that are self-perpetuating for fairly long periods of time. The unit method is not to be restricted to the intermediate grades, although it usually receives its most frequent use in this setting. Slow children in the primary grades do not have the necessary academic skills or maturity to participate fully in unit planning or to work independently on individual unit topics. The usual departmentalization of the junior and senior high schools make it difficult to implement the unit concept. Where secondary classes are homogeneous and meet for relatively large blocks of time, unit instruction is used commonly and effectively.

The intermediate grades provide an opportunity for the development of initial understandings in the areas of health and safety. Hopefully, the primary program, with family and community support, will have established basic habits that can be strengthened in later grades by developing an understanding of why those habits are important. It is appropriate in the intermediate grades to develop an awareness of the total involvement of the community in providing vital health and safety services, including an understanding of the family's role in using and maintaining these services. The grooming habits and self-care activities that play such a vital part in future job success are also given special emphasis at this time.

The intermediate curriculum should include continued attention to the development of academic skills, should provide the child with an opportunity to review necessary readiness skills, and should allow him to participate in remedial as well as developmental academic work. Those elements of the primary curriculum from which the slow learner would appear to gain continued profit should be brought forward and presented in keeping with the child's social level.

The use of auxilliary services for parental guidance and counseling should be continued in the intermediate grades. Care must be taken to see that concern for the child's slowness does not result in overprotection. Teacher guidance will include attention to the parents' questions and fears associated with the child's development and to their growing concern for his vocational future.

In summary, it may be said that the early intermediate grades generally conclude the sifting-out period during which those slow learners who are actually mentally retarded, emotionally disturbed, minimally brain injured, culturally deprived, or placed in a category more suitable than slow learning are no longer educated as slow but are given a program matched to their needs. The intermediate curriculum may facilitate the process by including testing activities and by providing intensive remedial work for those children who appear ready to profit from the regular curriculum. At the intermediate level, specific curriculum provisions and procedures should be developed to meet the educational needs implied by slowness, rather than developing a curriculum designed merely to treat individual differences. Curriculum provisions for slow learners in the intermediate grades emphasize the consolidation of earlier academic gains and include the introduction of new subject matter appropriate to the child's growing academic skills. This is when the unit method will be used extensively to correlate subject matter. The intermediate school years are a period of review and remediation; they also signal the introduction of many new activities that will help prepare the child for later life adjustment. The intermediate curriculum provides opportunities for testing and screening. Hopefully, it also results in the grouping of children by their learning characteristics so that they may be ready to gain maximum benefit from the junior high school program that follows.

CURRICULUM DEVELOPMENT IN THE JUNIOR HIGH SCHOOL

The junior high school years—a time of turmoil for any child—are no less so for the slow learner. He has all the usual pressures and fears of the early teens, but he has far fewer resources for coping with them. The school's demands further complicate his harried existence, and they may so overwhelm him that his only recourse is to flee—through withdrawal, aggressiveness, or dropping out. Accordingly, the junior high school curriculum for the slow learner must have a format that includes familiar elements and contains a very clear statement of goals and requirements. The curriculum must help the teen identify and evaluate his present role in the school and his evolving role in the community; it must assist him to translate his feelings into avenues of acceptable communication, rather than into hostile actions. The junior high school curriculum must motivate the student to remain in school, and, at the same time, prepare him to meet life should he drop out at the legal leaving age.

At the junior high school level, the curriculum provides students with their final experiences in developmental academics. These experiences should be chosen carefully to echo previous skills while paving the way for the practical and applied academic subjects that, it is hoped, will comprise the major part of the high school curriculum. In planning academic experiences, the junior high school teacher faces a student who desires academic independence but is not quite ready to achieve it. He still requires considerable support, but this assistance must be supplied in ways that do not threaten his concept of himself as a relatively mature person who can make decisions on his own.

In addition to considering the usual teen problems, the junior high school curriculum will have to contend with the unfavorable student attitudes that result from continuous school failure. The teacher should start by making a careful study of the child's threshold of success and then follow through by providing many activities that can help the student achieve a sense of accomplishment. The activities should be brief and novel, and they should appear to be similar to the regular program. There are many new and exciting areas of study for the student in junior high school, and these should be capitalized upon when they appear to offer a challenge leading to success.

In addition to providing opportunities for success, the curriculum should include guidance and counseling activities oriented toward helping the student and his family accept failure and lowered educational and vocational aspirations. Much of the guidance activity can be related to the curriculum's emphasis on vocational exploration. This emphasis will be reflected in trips to various industries, observations of a number of work situations, discussions with the respective tradesmen and craftsmen, and studies of broad job families. These and similar activities should assist students in their efforts to learn the general dimensions of the world of work, even though they do not have the maturity to select their specific place in this world.

The curriculum must anticipate problems of behavior that grow out of learning frustration, difficulties in communication, and poor screening and placement procedures. The curriculum alone cannot be expected to provide the solutions for all of these problems, but it can help by being flexible, imaginative, and sensitive to students' interests and needs. The curriculum should also set limits that may be understood by the student. A great deal of disruptive adolescent behavior is testing behavior. If students know the limits of the curriculum, one area of possible testing and consequent disruption will be removed.

The junior high school curriculum may be characterized as being a transitional curriculum. It relates the specific educational materials of the preceding years to the specific educational demands of the years to follow. It is a very flexible curriculum, because it must meet a much wider span of ability than students have evidenced thus far. Yet, it is a curriculum that has well-established boundaries that help provide structure for the teen who is without a firm structure of his own. The academic emphasis leans toward terminating developmental activities while stressing remedial measures. A strong guidance emphasis is continued by focusing attention on future vocational choice. The success of the junior high school curriculum depends on teacher attitude rather than on subject content. This dependence, unfortunately, is the reason why the junior high school curriculum often appears to be ineffective.

CURRICULUM DEVELOPMENT IN THE SENIOR HIGH SCHOOL

The curriculum constants of the senior high school must be described even more generally than were those included in the junior high school. The general rigidity of the high school setting makes curriculum almost synonymous with grouping procedures and thus difficult to discuss unless the school's organizational pattern is known.

The high school curriculum should focus on education for family life and community responsibility. The life-centered curriculum appears to be the most appropriate, because the situations for which it seeks to prepare are close at hand. Because marriage often closely follows the student's vocational placement, education for this responsibility is essential. Consumer education is critical for the slow learner, whose somewhat limited earning potential will allow him little room for economic mistakes. The program should emphasize community agencies, particularly those that may assist him in vocational placement and adjustment. The slow learner needs an opportunity to practice his developing social skills under helpful guidance. Also, students should be given the required assistance to adjust to their families upon whom they still are dependent but beginning to outgrow.

Instruction in academics should be continued to the extent of the individual's willingness to participate. Remedial work should be undertaken where necessary. The teacher should be aware that impending vocational placement may give new purpose to the student's school experiences and may stimulate him to significant academic achievement. Some students will still be unable to perform academic tasks independently and will require a program of survival studies. This program will teach skills essential to vocational success and include specific attention to reading safety signs, making rapid change, telling time accurately, and following involved directions.

The school work-study program provides a logical conclusion to the high school curriculum. It should, however, be considered only a part of the secondary program and not the only choice available.

For those slow learners who reach high school, and many do not, the curriculum serves as a bridge between school and work. The adult world gradually impinges upon the content of the high school curriculum as the student moves toward vocational placement. It becomes the main focus of learning in the school work-study or similar programs. Social skills receive important emphasis in high school and serve to give purpose to academic learning. The high school curriculum generally results in homogeneous grouping. Nonetheless, students should learn school subjects with their peers when it is possible to promote such interaction without excessive frustration or psychic damage. Academic subjects are given a practical flavor but can be enjoyed also for the intellectual stimulation and sense of accomplishment they provide. The high school curriculum will be final in the sense that it is the last learning sequence encountered by the student, but it must not be final in that it signals an end to all his learning. It should challenge, stimulate, and beguile the slow learner to continue his quest for knowledge no matter how limited, through necessity, that quest may be.

SUMMARY

Curriculum development for the slow learner has basically the same sources and process as does general curriculum development. It differs in emphasis and it reflects a philosophy that realizes the demands of the learner as well as the traditions of society. In practice, three general curriculum approaches are employed. The first, the slow track approach, is quite similar to the traditional academic curriculum. The second, the life-centered approach, is derived from experimentalism and brings the slow learner into contact with situations planned to help him achieve better adjustment in later life. The third choice, the vocational curriculum, narrows life choices to the vocational area and provides very specific preparation. Each approach is nonexclusive of the other, and considerable overlapping is evident when any of them is implemented. Despite the variety of approaches available, common curriculum elements may be identified at the primary, intermediate, junior high, and senior high school level. In the primary program, extended readiness and careful growth in basic academic skills are curriculum touchstones. Consolidation of knowledge and the use of it to attack new content areas are prime features of the intermediate curriculum. The junior high school years are filled with turmoil and, thus, demand flexible curriculum planning. In the high school years, the curriculum provides specific preparation for meeting adult responsibilities. Whatever the instructional level, the curriculum takes on substance only when it is applied by an imaginative teacher and supported by an administrative plan that directs instruction to students with common learning problems.

CHAPTER VI

Subject Matter Adaptations

When a teacher faces one, several, or a group of slow students for the first time, his primary concern is how to provide activities that will stimulate learning and concurrently prevent discipline problems. Such is reality. Theoretical consideration of screening procedures, grouping plans, and over-all curriculum design are extremely important. Rarely, however, does a teacher enter an instructional setting where these concerns have been thoroughly implemented. For most teachers, the quest for a well-ordered, philosophically correct curriculum begins with an urgent need for "something to do." The planning of programs in response to immediate pressures is not especially wise but may be especially necessary. Many educators decry the use of "educational recipes" and the proliferation of instructional "cook books." However, recognizing the fact that recipes have a place in every kitchen where they can provide quick sustenance if not immediate creativity, this chapter provides specific teaching suggestions in those subject areas where such suggestions are available. The suggestions are drawn from observation, reports from various teachers of slow learners, experience with the educable mentally retarded, and literature on classroom suggestions for slow learners.

It is expected that teachers will scrutinize these suggestions carefully and relate them to the context of the curriculum that they use. Many of these adaptations result from one teacher's experience with one class, the composition of which has usually been indefinitely described. Very few suggestions have been subjected to careful research scrutiny. It is hoped that the ideas included will provide the beginning teacher with starting points from which he must grow, and that they will provide the experienced teacher with a basis for comparing his familiar methods to those used with slow learners. Further, it is hoped that a review of the literature on adaptations will stimulate the development of appropriate methods and materials in all subject areas. The ensuing discussion is seen, then, merely as a framework that the teacher is encouraged to strengthen and extend.

BASIC ASSUMPTIONS

The method most often used for adapting standard instructional content to slow learning is that of slowing the rate of presentation. Several other adaptations that may be equally useful in instructional planning for slow learners are: reducing the content of the material in volume and complexity, altering emphasis of material to match immediate interests, replacing abstract illustrations with more concrete ones, expanding background material so that the student has a greater basis for understanding, replacing an approach of listening and looking with one of doing and reporting, presenting the material in ways that involve more than one sensory pathway to learning, enlivening the standard sequence through novel methods of introducing materials, using pretesting activities to give the teacher specific information on what the child knows.

Adaptations should be based on materials or approaches that have proved effective with normal students. Poor materials will not improve in quality simply because they are used with poor learners. The normal or bright learner may achieve in spite of poor materials or approaches; the slow learner certainly will not be able to overcome this additional handicap.

When developing methodological approaches in one subject matter area, the teacher should bear in mind the effects these adaptations will have in other subject matter areas. This principle will be applied quite easily in the elementary school where the teacher has a knowledge of the total curriculum; but it may be impossible to apply this principle consistently in the secondary school where instruction is fragmented by subject matter specialization. While the secondary level teacher cannot ensure correlations between subjects, he can provide for consistency within his own subject matter specialty.

Instructional methods should be planned to introduce and carry forward some definite subject content. In many cases, the methods prescribed for slow learners become ends in themselves and little attention is given to content. This is particularly true of audiovisual aids, field trips, and manual activities. These and other methods are very useful in adapting subject matter, but they are not automatically successful. In fact, to be beneficial, the use of special methods requires considerably more time and careful planning than do more conventional teaching methods.

One of the major sources of teaching adaptations for slow learners is the field of mental retardation. However, materials that have been used with the mentally retarded are not always appropriate for use with slow learners since these materials reflect specific learning characteristics and an educational philosophy that cannot be transferred easily. Materials for the retarded may move too slowly, foster more dependence than should be encouraged in slow learners, be difficult to apply in any but a special class setting, and have a social orientation that tends to demean a slow learner. Although their availability makes their use tempting, methods and materials for the retarded must be chosen carefully and be adapted to the slow learner's characteristics and needs. Since many materials developed for the retarded do not have to pass the more stringent requirements or face the commercial competition of most materials developed for normal children, they may be instructionally inferior even though they are popular.

The teacher should include some way of testing his methods or materials when he draws up initial plans to use them. Evaluation may include the traditional measures of content learned, may be a systematic recording of student reactions, may involve teaching in one manner to one group while teaching the same material in a different manner to a second but similar group, or may be planned as a joint venture of two or more teachers. If the teacher is trying a method that is described in the literature or observed in another classroom, he should know the conditions under which it was originally applied so that the similarities or differences of his approach and their possible effect on the learner may be evaluated.

The term "slow learning" is not specific enough to be used in planning adaptations for groups of learners. When an adaptation is made, it will be maximally effective only with some slow learners. Other members of the slow group must be reached in other ways. Thus, each adaptation must be supplemented with small group or individual activities chosen to meet the needs of those students who are not reached through the primary learning experience.

The teacher who has studied and modified these basic assumptions to fit his teaching situation is ready to consider the content adaptations that they underlie.

ART AND CRAFT ACTIVITIES

Art and craft activities have traditionally been seen by the classroom teacher as one of several subject areas that afford the slow learner an opportunity for success and provide him a respite from the pressures of academic learning. Artistic skill is often seized upon eagerly and may be promoted as a vocational goal. The art specialist, for one, may not share this view of the importance of art and craft activities for slow learners and may seek to protect what he considers to be the integrity of the art curriculum. As Venable [154] notes, "Art is becoming to education what the hall closet is to home. In it we stuff all of our leftover or unwanted items, then forget they exist."

Actually, art and craft instruction has many facets and phases and should not be considered solely as a "relief" activity by the regular teacher nor as an academic discipline by the art specialist. The classroom teacher who adopts this philosophy of balanced emphasis is better able to plan a comprehensive art program and may be able to assist the art specialist in adapting his instruction to meet the slow student's specific needs.

Art can be a very valuable means of expression for the slow learner, but, like his other means of communication, its quality may be somewhat limited. He will better express his feelings about himself and his environment if he is allowed to build from his everyday observations. In addition to working with the ideas drawn from his immediate surroundings, he should be encouraged to observe and re-create unfamiliar worlds. The slow student has difficulty abstracting, remembering, and associating ideas, and he must be carefully prepared for every observation. He will be helped by being given a preview of pictorial and verbal clues and by having an opportunity for immediate discussion of his findings. He will need assistance in sorting the major and minor features of the observed situation, and the experience should not be so extensive that the slow learner cannot absorb the necessary ideas in the time allowed. If these elements are included in the observation situation and the student's reaction to them is assessed carefully, they may be relaxed considerably as the student grows in his power to observe.

The teacher who is often unable to understand a child's verbal productions should not succumb to the temptation to read a great deal into his artistic ones. The interpretation of paintings, clay modeling, and other art work is somewhat inconclusive, even when practiced by persons highly trained and experienced in its techniques. It is not a field for amateurs, even those with the best intentions.

There is no reason why the slow learner should be denied use of any artistic media or technique that is appropriate to his mental and dexterity levels. When the slow learner injures himself or destroys valuable materials, it is usually because the teacher assumed certain skills rather than testing them in activities that gradually increase in difficulty. Also, the slow student may not have the reading ability to follow printed directions on material containers that the regular student uses without conscious thought. Some students can transform a spilled jar of paint into an art masterpiece. Slow learners do not often see creative alternatives to their artistic mistakes. They may not have the imagination to do so, or they have learned from experience in other subject matter areas that teachers do not generally reward incorrect deviations no matter how creative they may be.

Instruction in most craft activities should include a presentation of a finished product or a representative model. This technique will assist students to realize the specific purpose the project serves and how difficult its completion will be. It is essential to plan step-by-step demonstrations and to provide the students with opportunities to practice, if only mentally, the techniques of each step. Examples of the current project will help provide motivation, particularly if the objects displayed were made by students whose general skill level is known to the slow learner. Samples, of course, allow for copying and tend to stifle creativity. If the teacher uses a variety of samples and removes them during the actual work periods, the copying problem can be alleviated. String painting, scrap printing, junk assemblage, stick printing, random paper cutting, and similar activities that almost always result in original productions should be included frequently. These activities help students develop expressive freedom without fear that they will be measured in terms of how far they deviate from an existing model.

The art program should have creative as well as practical and therapeutic value. One route to creativity may be pursued by considering various materials in terms of their basic properties and the results that occur when these properties are altered. For example, a paper plate is round, concave, easily cut, easily glued or stapled, usually divided into several concentric circles by its markings, easily colored (if not the waxed type), and rather light in weight. The center of a paper plate can be simply decorated with crayon, chalk, or paper applique, its high rim serving as a suitable frame. Two plates can be laced together, filled with beans, and decorated with tempera or crayon to become a shaker. One and one-half plates can be decorated and laced or stapled together to form a holder for letters or potholders. Two plates with their centers cut out can be stapled together at the edges and wrapped with green crepe paper to become a wreath. Two plates similarly treated except for wrapping can become a stained-glass window by gluing colored cellophane and strips of black paper over the center openings. An unusual scene is created when the center is cut from one plate, the hole covered inside with clear plastic wrap, and the resulting window stapled to another whole plate, the intact inside of which has been decorated with crayons, cotton clouds, and a forest of small twigs. Two plates, stapled together at the edges and covered with metal foil, create a flying saucer with headlights when a few bright beads are pinned or laced to the top and rim. A very suitable spaceman results when two pair of joined plates are attached one above the other, a face and buttons of colored paper are glued on, and gloved hands and booted feet of construction paper are added by stapling. A basket is made by scoring a plate one-third off center on both sides and drawing the sides together with ribbon or string. A single plate drawn up and together at the sides also becomes the body for a number of animals such as a bear or, when not drawn so tightly, a turtle. When the basic form is slit on both sides, the resulting fan shape at one end forms the base for a simple turkey. A plate colored yellow, given a black paper center, and scalloped deeply at the edges becomes a suitable sunflower or daisy. These are just a few of the many ideas that illustrate the creative projects that are possible if the teacher first considers the material rather than adapts the material to well-stylized ideas.

Art and craft activities are not taught as sequentially as other subjects in the curriculum and consequently must be matched carefully to the students' interests and general developmental skills. In the primary grades, art activities will be a very important outlet for the child's expression. They will help him gain needed practice in color recognition, form perception, and other activities related to reading readiness. And, they should provide the child with experiences in developing the self-discipline so necessary to following directions and completing tasks. Lessons at the primary level should be informal, be as long as the child's developing interest permits, and should emphasize the pleasure of the experience. Activities that require memorization of rules, exacting exercises, or extensive use of verbal or mathematical skills should not be included in a program for the primary age slow learner. He still functions at a general readiness level and needs time to explore art as a new learning activity.

In the intermediate grades, art and craft materials become more numerous because the child is rapidly developing the maturity and dexterity necessary for dealing with them. He is now creating objects that are designed to fulfill a purpose. His earlier "accidents" that became finger bowls for small fingers are now at least the result of conscious effort. The slow learner is making many projects that grow out of his unit studies and observations from his surroundings. He is beginning to establish an art and craft vocabulary of spoken and written words. He is reading simple directions and beginning to work from simple plans.

The junior high school years see some art activity in the home classroom in terms of special unit projects or holiday decorations.

However, most artistic products emerge from the student's art classes with a special art teacher. He will probably be in the lower sections of the art program, although he should be grouped by his artistic ability rather than by his general ability. If he does show any special talents, these should be encouraged and as much special instruction as possible should be provided. In many cases, art production in the junior high will reflect immediate interests in cars, violence, and modern folk heros such as Batman. This is a facet of expression that should not be entirely discouraged. These interests may be used as a starting point to develop an eventual appreciation of beauty, form, order, and other elements that can help the student find structure and meaning in his environment.

The slow student is often lost in the rather specialized world of high school art instruction. He need not be if art instruction includes a general orientation to vocations, consumer education, and other matters of immediate interest. The slow student with talent should not be fooled by its seemingly attractive vocational potential; the art world is extremely competitive and demands far more than the good drafting skill that is often interpreted to be excellent artistic production. An art interest and talent in high school may lead to an exploration of art and art-related vocations, but only in unusual cases should hopes of achieving a career in creative or commercial art be fostered in the student and his parents.

Art is important as a subject and as a general activity throughout the slow student's school career. Its many facets should be explored with each student. Its pleasures should become his.

BUSINESS EDUCATION

In the over-all curriculum of the average secondary school, business subjects are another area where large numbers of slow students are traditionally found. As Calhoun [157] notes, "Because general business is regarded as general education for all students the business teacher often finds a more heterogeneous group than that encountered in the area of the skills." This rather mild introduction to a nettlesome problem is typical of the very positive manner in which business teachers describe their attempts to meet the needs of the slow student. The literature indicates that these attempts begin with a careful analysis of the place the slow student is expected to assume in the business community. Eyster [160] suggests that the standard business course that prepares typists, stenographers, bookkeepers, and other skilled office personnel might better shift its emphasis to a general clerical and sales orientation. He feels that the slow student can do well in these areas if he has developed a positive employment orientation and is well grounded in common general skills.

Perry [167] specifies that duplicating, stock work, general office work, and general clerical sales are examples of positions in which business will accept a "plodder." Perry also stresses a program of preparation that will build general work skills and positive work attitudes. Krawitz [166], echoing the statements of previous authors, places emphasis on the role of the individual teacher in considering alternate training and placement plans for the slow student. In discussing placement of slow students, Shows [172] makes the interesting point that, since the slow learner may find security and a lack of pressure in routine jobs, he may actually be considered to have a special ability since workers who enjoy routinization are difficult to find. The assumption on which this suggestion is based is, of course, open to question; there is little research evidence to verify it. The use of follow-up studies, another suggestion by Shows, would appear to shed more light on this and similar problem areas.

One method of preparing slow business students is suggested by Brown [156], who would divide the business program into two tracks. The first track would include all students with an I.Q. above 95 and would stress preparation for specific business occupations. The second track would include all slow learners with an I.Q. below 95 (presumably no lower than 75) and would stress general occupational preparation for lower level office jobs. There is no discussion of the fact that many studies in the field of retardation show very little relationship between job success and specific I.Q. scores [Goldstein and Heber, 182].

Several authors feel that the slow learner can gain particular benefit from learning in simulated business situations [Krawitz, 165; Ellenbogen, 159]. The simulation allows students to gain experience with various office machines in a setting that has some of the demands and pressures of an actual business. In addition to this suggestion, business teachers indicate success with methods that accept student differences; present materials in short, carefully controlled lessons; build a specific business vocabulary; stress audiovisual approaches; provide varied repetition; eliminate fear and develop confidence; stress personality development; and key instruction to lower reading and arithmetic achievement levels. A rather complete description of a two-year program that incorporates these suggestions is given by Ellenbogen [159]. The author advocates that during the first semester attention should be given to building an interest in work and to introducing terms and concepts of clerical work. The program should move to projects that require students to follow simple instructions and complete tasks such as taking telephone messages, writing invoices, and recording orders. During the second year of study, the student is introduced to business machines in a simulated office setting. Students move between office stations on the basis of their accomplishments. Typing is studied during both years. Rothchild [169] describes a similar program in Clearwater, Florida.

While most authors stress a general approach to the business curriculum for slow students, several have given attention to individual subjects. Haga [162] suggests ways in which standard texts may be revised to develop maximum understanding and skill in simplified bookkeeping. Haga's methods include using the adding machine for operations usually done by hand, using simplified journal forms, and working with actual forms in presenting problems such as payroll deductions.

House [164] suggests that achievement in bookkeeping is related closely to improvement in reading skills. House asks the teacher to include attention to technical vocabulary, be aware of the student's exact reading level, preview reading assignments, stress the use of illustrations, provide summary questions and study guides, give more attention to discussion sessions, rely less on texts, and de-emphasize reading in the testing program. Satlow [170] describes a system for developing bookkeeping materials that are highly sequential and move forward in small steps. His system utilizes a series of problems that gradually increase in difficulty. He gives careful attention to reading and arithmetic competence, and he involves students in the development of materials that are duplicated for class use. Henderson [163] argues that bookkeeping should be included in the curriculum for slow learners. The results of his follow-up study indicate that, while slower bookkeeping students were unable to perform complicated bookkeeping tasks, their skills helped them to find and hold a business position. Wolters [174] reports on a grouping plan used to solve the problem of individual differences in heterogeneous bookkeeping classes. Wolter's groups have a student leader and secretary and are under the over-all supervision of a student office manager. Each group moves through the text at its own rate. Students choose their own group with the understanding that they must meet its achievement standards. Austin [155] also used groups in a program built around the bookkeeping practice set.

Shotak [171] describes methods for developing shorthand skills that can be used with slow learners at upper achievement and adjustment levels. Sierles [199] suggests that economics be programmed for the slow learner. His description and application of programmed learning, however, is quite nonspecific.

Feather [161] uses a series of graduated problems to teach typing skills to slower students. Problems drawn from the text are presented on duplicated sheets; students are expected to solve each problem correctly and move to the next. The system is said to be effective because it keeps all students occupied, provides incentive without frustration, and eases the teacher's "paper work" burden. Plymire [168] suggests that slower typing students will be helped if timed tests are postponed until minimum skills are developed, failing grades are eliminated, and initial steps receive considerable repetition.

Teaching business subjects to the slow student is generally considered appropriate as long as instruction is closely related to placement opportunities. The business positions generally held by slow learners demand few highly developed skills, but they do require a willing worker who has a general orientation to, and interest in, the world of business. There are very few original or highly specialized techniques to be found in business education, as instruction appears to be based on the same assumptions that predicate methodology in other subject areas. Automation and programming have greatly affected business procedures but have had little effect on business education for slow learners. Although the effects of automation on the future place of the slow learner in the business world is hinted at in literature, it has not received the extensive treatment in terms of its implications for business preparation programs. The literature on teaching business subjects to slow learners suggests a definite need for extensive communication between high school business teachers and teachers at the elementary and junior high levels. It appears that many activities included in business education are central to general vocational success and must be given early attention. Such activities include alphabetization, money skills, letter writing, filling in forms, and general attention to detail. Because the business teacher is closer to the reality of the work world, he can more easily and accurately identify these skills and pass on some teaching tips to the staff of the elementary school.

COMMUNICATION

When discussing communication skills, it is necessary to depart from the subject matter organization used in the previous sections since, in this content area there is considerable overlapping among the subjects of reading, spelling, writing, speaking, English, literature, dramatics, and grammar. Consequently it is important to discuss the composite topic of communication skills rather than giving attention to individual subjects.

Verbal Language. Throughout the slow learner's school career, his basic communication problems are frequently traceable to inadequate verbal language. Strom [78] notes:

> One often finds that the maximum exposure to language has come from the television set, a situation in which the pupil is exposed to torrents of language used in situations unfamiliar to him. In addition, no response is expected of him; he is merely an observer not a participant in the communication process.

The slow child's verbal deficiencies are not always caused by "televisionitis." The specific problem will vary with the type of child being discussed. The culturally deprived slow learner has a rich verbal language, but its content is generally considered to be inappropriate to the school setting. Conversely, the constitutionally slow learner will not have the verbal capacity expected of a child his chronological age and may not be ready to profit from the language experiences received. A final example of differences in causation is the slow learner with emotional difficulties who may have sufficient language capacity but be unable to achieve enough environmental rapport to use this capacity in an acceptable manner.

Whatever causes verbal language deficiencies, the slow child's school experiences clearly should be based in language development. At the primary level, the slow learner must receive specific help and motivation to discover and name persons and objects in his environment and to describe relationships between them. His spoken vocabulary should prepare him to cope with reading, writing, and other school vocabularies he is expected to master. He must be taught the many subtle shadings of classroom language, know their meaning, and learn the choice of appropriate verbal responses. The teacher, too, must learn to listen. Too often, teachers are unaware of what the child can say.

It is in the intermediate grades that the standard teaching emphasis shifts from development to embellishment. The slow learner, however, still requires intensive experience in listening, verbal expression, and translation of spoken words into writing. In the intermediate years, when cumulative school failure will affect the incentive to learn, language instruction must have specific meaning for the slow student. Alexander [175] recommends that oral expression be derived from school activities in which the child has succeeded. The tape recorder, a class T.V. studio, a class clubhouse, and similar devices may be used to build environmentally based language that is school related. The intermediate level teacher of the culturally deprived slow learner must pay particular attention to nonverbal language and to language that has a specific cultural base. Such language plays an increasingly important part in the growing child's environmental communication and should be considered in planning school language programs. The child's nonschool language may be extremely important to the defense structure he has erected against middle class intrusions into his life. The teacher should build on the child's environmental language rather than subjugate or eliminate it.

Social language is increasingly important in the secondary school years as the student prepares for his adult role. This language includes a work vocabulary that is built gradually as the pupil moves toward leaving school. The proportion of verbally based school activities continues to be considerably greater than those planned for normal students as the spoken word is still the slow learner's most useful communication tool. This fact requires curriculum adjustments in subject areas that depend traditionally upon well-developed reading and writing skills. These adjustments should be directed to activity-oriented projects that motivate verbal expression. A more talkative teacher is not a recommended adjustment.

Reading. The adequate development of the slow learner's verbal language is an end in itself and is related closely to the development of an effective reading program. Authorities on reading for slow learners consistently recommend that reading materials be developed by the teacher from the language that children use in talking about what they do [Gates, 180; Strang, 201; Sullivan, 203].

The young slow learner usually begins to read a year or more after the normal child and requires readiness activities until age seven or eight [Schonell, 197; Strang, 201]. The teacher's careful analysis of all readiness factors and the individual child's expression of interest in reading will determine the exact age at which formal instruction should begin. The factor on which this decision depends is whether or not the child is able to make the transition from exercises in symbol recognition to the full integration of reading symbols without consistent and obvious failure.

The readiness materials and approaches employed will be planned largely in response to a careful study of each child. The slow pupil often develops very unevenly thus necessitating a considerable revision or repetition of the recommended readiness sequence. A unique aspect of extended readiness is that activities must be planned for a higher than usual social and interest level. The seven- or eight-year-old slow learner cannot be approached as though he were still five or six. Another special use of readiness materials is that they may have to be applied in a remedial manner in the intermediate or junior high school years when students show evident gaps in the skills necessary to reading success.

The slow learner shares with all children a keen initial interest in the magical subject of reading. This interest is dulled somewhat by the long readiness period and can be extinguished completely unless the initial and continuing phases of instruction are stimulating, actively involve the learner, and provide for earned success.

Early reading instruction should be systematic. There is no one instructional approach that research supports as being particularly effective with slow learners. There is evidence that consistency is extremely important in using a single method or in transferring elements from one method to another. The slow learner is often handicapped in developing his reading skills by changes in methodology that result from either the teacher's need to see success or from the fact that the slow learner may be taught by two or three teachers during the extended time in which he develops his basic reading skills. To help teachers maintain consistency, the approaches that are tried and discarded should be carefully recorded. The suspected reasons for the failure of a particular approach should be given in every case.

Slow learners develop word-attack skills more efficiently if instruction is based on words in their spoken vocabulary and is oriented to the recognition of syllables and small words rather than to the analysis of individual sounds [Epler, 179; Strang, 201]. Effective teaching of word-attack skills also seems to depend on making word recognition part of a continuous process so that experiences prior to the lesson give the child a foundation on which to base his understanding of the lesson material [Justa, 184].

Reading instruction for slow learners at all stages will depend heavily on teacher-prepared materials and materials developed from the students' experiences. In many cases, the duplicator and various adaptations of the experience chart will supplement or replace basal texts and workbooks. The teacher interested in exploring additional avenues of learning should consider using tactile-kinesthetic procedures. These procedures are described by McCarthy and Oliver [192] in a review of the Fernald method and other kinesthetic techniques. The Fernald method requires the child to choose his own vocabulary; he learns to read this vocabulary by tracing the letters while saying them. He transfers individual words to scratch paper and then incorporates them into a written story. The story is typed and read again in print. Individual words are filed on cards in alphabetical order for later reference or review. Tracing continues only until reading is established. Other methods described by McCarthy and Oliver include the construction of words from sandpaper letters or other letters that are large and sharply textured, assembling words using cardboard letters of various colors, building letters from rolled-out strips of clay, writing in a pan of salt or a box of wet sand, painting letters or words on large sheets of paper, cutting traced letters and pasting them on paper to make words, rubbing crayon on paper over sandpaper letters, using blocks with sentence-building words on their sides, sprinkling sand over letters that have been painted on paper with glue, and tracing letters or words that are thrown on a screen by the process of rear projection. Kinesthetic techniques are designed to be integrated into a total program of reading instruction. They demand an imaginative teacher who can plan class grouping and routines so that each child may receive the individual attention the techniques require.

The problems of primary-level reading instruction center around the slow learner's experience gaps, his relatively poor ability to make abstractions, and his consequent need for an extended period of readiness and initial instruction. Despite these problems, the slow learner's reading abilities can be developed to or near their maximum potential through a carefully planned program taught by a teacher who has a positive but realistic expectation of success. Despite his difficulties, the primary-age slow child participates in the same kind of activities as do other children of his age. He feels important because he attends school, is learning, and is generally well-accepted by his classmates.

The intermediate years bring a new dimension to reading instruction. Reading increasingly becomes the child's primary tool for learning. As the slow learner finds he is unable to meet the new demands, he begins to feel shut off from the books and materials used by faster learners. His inability to compete may increase his feeling of being different and heighten his sensitivity to rejection from teachers and fellow students. Although there are no formulas for reducing the efforts of failure, this task is the teacher's greatest challenge in the school's middle years. He must help the child overcome failure before failure overwhelms the child. Deceptive marking does not help, nor does unearned praise. The teacher must provide class activities that logically include the slower pupil and provide a range of responses that include his ability level. The teacher must, if possible, set aside more time for the slow child or obtain individual remedial reading instruction for him. The teacher may have to give occasional indulgence to the slow pupil's need for peer status by assigning books that will not be read or homework that cannot be done; but the teacher must always bring the child back to reality in the protected privacy of individual work sessions or conferences. The school's middle years are the most difficult for the slow learner; it is during this time that his cumulative failure begins to negate any feeling of success that his school activities may provide.

In terms of specific reading instruction, the intermediate grades are a period in which the slow learner begins to consolidate his reading skills and gain independence in reading. Every classroom should feature an attractive library corner containing books that are short and simple. Books should be changed frequently so that pupils do not lose interest in their contents. The immediate access to books provided by the library corner should be supplemented by visits to the school library and the public library. The books chosen by students should, if possible, be incorporated into the classroom reading program. The slow learner may be motivated to read on his own through membership in a reading club or by keeping a log of the books he has read.

Grouping for reading instruction may or may not be used in the primary grades. It is, however, an essential element of the intermediate program where the range of individual abilities is increasingly noticeable. The number of reading groups usually recommended is three, but they may vary according to the composition of the class, the teacher's ability to organize instruction, and the reasons for grouping. Children may be grouped according to their reading ability, their reading interests, or the specific skill to be developed [Clark, 177]. Whatever the number of groups or the basis for revised grouping, the procedures should be flexible and sensitive to conditions requiring change.

Some children in the intermediate grades will still be in the beginning stages of reading and will require work on experience charts. Such charts may now take on the guise of the class newspaper, trip notebooks, current events folders, and the like. It is important that the child does not reject the experience method because it is presented in a way that appears babyish. In order to facilitate learning through experience, Lee and Allen [187] suggest that several interest centers be organized in the classroom. These centers will provide a number of activities that may stimulate individual or group experience stories. Among the centers mentioned are those devoted to writing, music, art, science, and publishing.

The range of reading abilities at the intermediate level may be so great as to negate any attempts at grouping. Or, disturbed behavior accompanying slow learning may make grouping unwise until the disturbed individuals gain enough inner security to work with others. In either case, the teacher may wish to use a program of individualized reading. In this approach, those children who do not fit into the usual grouping pattern or who would appear to benefit from individualized instruction are given a carefully planned program of reading selections and related activities that help them master reading skills on their own. A number of authors have given extensive attention to this approach, and the teacher is referred to the following books for additional information:

Darrow, Helen Fischer, and Virgil M. Howes. *Approaches to Individualized Reading* (New York: Appleton-Century-Crofts, 1960).

Miel, Alice (ed.) *Individualizing Reading Practices* (New York: Teachers College Press, 1956).

Veatch, Jeanette. *Individualizing Your Reading Program* (New York: Putnam, 1959).

The slow learner in the intermediate school is beyond the stage where reading is undertaken for its own interest and excitement. Reading must have a purpose that he considers important; it must relate to his surroundings and to the interests of his age level. The teacher should consider using the growing number of books prepared specifically for urban youth and the several recent supplementary reading series that are humorous in nature (see Appendix A). Teachers should not ignore the value of collecting stories that are written by normal and slow students in the class. These stories may be compiled and duplicated. Current events, as presented in some mass-circulation newspapers and magazines, may be within the slower child's reading ability, as are the popular supplementary readers developed from materials appearing in *The Readers Digest* (see Appendix A).

Reading tends to lose its identity as a subject matter specialty in the junior and senior high schools. However, it does not lose its importance. The need to develop and maintain reading skills is a recurrent theme in all subject areas. Secondary school teachers who work with slow learners soon realize that their effectiveness in teaching subject matter content may depend to a large degree on their ability to impart a specialized vocabulary and other skills directly related to reading.

English is one of the subjects in which the continuation of reading instruction is most apparent. In the elementary school, the specific phonetic analysis of sounds is generally considered too difficult to be profitable for the slow learner. So, too, in the junior and senior high schools, the specific analysis of grammar is considered to be somewhat unimportant. Alexander [175] reports that slow students are interested in inspecting their own sentences for obvious errors in construction and word usage, but they are not interested in grammar per se. Only the basic and most fundamental grammar necessary for good usage in daily life should be covered because of the slow child's difficulty in abstraction [Shehan, 198]. Emphasis should be placed on the use of short sentences as these are easier for students to construct and correct [Leo, 188].

The usual stress on grammar and other formal English instruction is replaced in some schools by a program based on material drawn from the students' environment. Particular attention is given to problems of adult adjustment. Television, magazines, newspapers, and other mass media offer many instructional experiences. Teachers' approaches to using mass media vary from including it as one topical unit of the over-all English curriculum [Alexander, 175] to planning a special curriculum where mass media is a constant tool of instruction [Tincher, 205]. The medium of television is recommended for motivation by Leo [188] who states, "Rarely can lower ability classes be expected to read a play outside of class; nonetheless, plays should be studied because of their importance on television." Keyes [185] uses media reports of the academy awards and discussions of television series to introduce creative dramatics to his class.

An interesting method of incorporating the environment into instruction is reported by Greene [183]. His class visited its neighborhood and compiled a list of the conditions observed. After discussion, the class wrote letters to neighborhood residents and merchants commending some and reminding others of the various problems that their premises presented. The replies were read in class and provoked additional discussion. The environment within the school also offers many opportunities for English experiences. Leven [190] describes on-going school situations such as the student council meetings and the junior prom where practical English may be used. Alexander [175] mentions the use of experiences in other school subjects, such as shop or cooking, as the basis for oral expression and writing.

Most secondary school English programs for slow learners are conducted by teachers interested primarily in the more academically inclined students. These teachers may work with slow learners for only several periods a week and cannot be expected to develop radically new approaches. This assumption is supported by the literature which includes a number of adaptations based in traditional subject matter. A mainstay of the high school English curriculum is the continuation of the traditions of a cultured society by exposing the students to classical literature. Zamchick [207] argues for the continuation of this tradition through the use of good reading in paperback form. Lobdell [191] describes a project that achieved the twin goals of introducing classical literature and improving reading skills by the use of an abridged edition of *A Tale of Two Cities.* Well-known dramatic productions are used by Goldberg [181] to stimulate the imagination of his slow learners through actively involving them in the learning experience. Ebbitt [178] has students read plays that reflect common experiences of the group—experiences that are not necessarily drawn from the immediate environment. During the reading, the cast is shifted several times so that "hopeless" readers will not be embarrassed.

Despite the representative references cited above, experienced teachers of slow learners question the value of traditional program content no matter how it is adapted. These doubts are summed up by Yarborough [206]:

> Since the slow learner usually confines his free-choice reading to newspapers and magazines, modern selections are more appropriate to him than classical ones. Of course, his tastes should be developed and his selection of reading materials carefully supervised, but many of the traditional literary selections are inappropriate for the slow learner.

Despite the apparent dissatisfaction with English subject matter adaptations, they continue because traditional materials are available while special materials are extremely difficult to find. One hopeful sign is the effort being made by local associations of English teachers to develop new materials. This effort is exemplied by the activities of the New Jersey Association of Teachers of English [194]. It is expected that teachers may find similar assistance from professional associations in their local areas.

The slow learner is considerably behind his normal peers in the frequency with which he uses reading as a major tool of communication. Yet, reading is of vital importance to him and demands careful instruction at all school levels. The slow child will require extended reading readiness that is accompanied by the continuous assessment of gaps in his experience and understanding. The teacher must prepare a large proportion of the child's early reading materials, and, during this process, he must consider the child's social and intellectual development. In the middle school years, considerable effort must be expended to prevent reading from becoming the focus of failure. Also, in these years, attention must be directed to developing the child's interest and facility in independent reading. Formal reading instruction is still of vital importance in junior and senior high school, although it may be sublimated to other concerns. Since so few teachers at the secondary level have time or training to teach reading, increased attention should be given to the development and use of self-testing or auto-instructional materials and to the possibility of using remedial specialists.

The teaching of reading, at all levels, is often handicapped by the lack of suitable reading materials; this need is particularly noticeable when the teacher seeks basic supplementary materials with a controlled vocabulary or looks for books that students may read for pleasure. Recognizing the need, several individuals and organizations have prepared lists of materials that are simply written yet have a high interest level. A representative sample of these publications is listed below.

Baum, Alice. *Your Reading,* National Council of Teachers of English, 704 South Sixth Street, Champaign, Illinois, 1960.
A book list for junior high school. Division of interest levels. Annotated. General indication of reading level.

Best Books for Children, R. R. Bowker Company, 62 West 45th Street, New York, 10036.
This is a yearly publication that does not specifically list books for slow learners but is extremely useful in checking the quality of books recommended through other sources.

Bibliography of Graded Books, Rocky Mountain School Study Council, Committee on Exceptional Children, Bureau of Research, University of Denver, Denver, Colorado, 1964.
High Interest–Low Vocabulary. A list of titles. No annotations. Gives interest level, vocabulary level by grade, author, publication date, and approximate price. Titles should serve as resource for review only. Available directly from the Council.

Crosby, Muriel, and Beatrice Hurley. *Adventuring with Books,* Champaign, Illinois: National Council of Teachers of English, 1960.
Topically arranged, annotated, and graded list.

Dunn, Anita. *Fare for the Reluctant Reader,* Capital Area School Development Association, State University of New York, Albany, New York, 1964.
Includes lists of magazines, remedial texts, and book lists.

How-To-Do-It Books, New York: R. R. Bowker, 1963.
A very large list of books on recreational and nonvocational subjects. Arranged by reading levels.

Reading List of High Interest–Low Vocabulary Books for Enriching Various Areas of the Curriculum, Storrs, Connecticut: University of Connecticut, Reading-Study Center, School of Education, no date.
A straight list of suggested titles. No annotations are provided, but general grade levels are given. Copies are available by writing the University of Connecticut.

Spache, George. *Good Reading for Poor Readers,* Champaign, Illinois: Garrard Publishers, 1964.

Strang, Ruth. *Gateways to Readable Books,* New York: H. W. Wilson, 1958.

Sullivan, Helen. *High Interest–Low Vocabulary Reading Materials,* Boston, Massachusetts: Boston University, School of Education, 1956.
Over 1,000 titles for specified reading levels.

Textbooks in Print, R. R. Bowker Company, March, 1966.
An inexpensive condensation of *Books in Print, Textbooks in Print* is an excellent source for ordering information on publishers and prices.

"The Index to Reading Materials," *Elementary English,* 40:106–109 (January, 1963).
A source list for high interest–low vocabulary books that is brought up to date every few years.

Zion, Mary Jo. *Bibliography of Reading Lists for Retarded Readers,* State University of Iowa Extension Bulletin No. 766, College of Education Series No. 38, Iowa City, Iowa, 1960.
Available directly from the State University. Includes about 100 sources of available book lists.

The teacher is referred also to Appendix A of this publication where he will find the specific titles of books that may be used with the slow learner in subject matter instruction. The teacher should also check his local library, local colleges and universities, and state departments of education for similar lists. Large city libraries and college departments of English, special education, and elementary education often prepare book lists that are oriented to specific localities.

Spelling. The spelling program for slow learners contains no methodological specialties. It will be more effective if the teacher remembers that, although English is not a truly phonetic language, people tend to spell words as they sound, and the slow learner may often use unusual pronunciation. As a result, his spelling may actually appear correct to him. A good spelling program should stress words the child uses in conversation and is likely to use in his future written communications. It should be remembered that the written production of the slow learner will probably be limited to letter writing and simple work records. Spelling instruction must be very systematic, frequent, and allow a number of opportunities for interesting repetition. Student involvement in spelling is important and may be gained by self-competition (word lists, common-error notebook) or through class competition (spelling games, spelling contests). Of course, the group competition should not be undertaken if the slow child has little expectation of success. The understanding and proper use of spelling words should be incorporated into each spelling lesson. Since the slow student tends to forget quickly what he does not use, the spelling program should provide many opportunities for application and review of the words learned. In addition to drawing words from the child's spoken vocabulary, the teacher should include spelling words that the child will need in other subjects, such as home economics, industrial arts, and the social studies.

Writing. Legibility is the primary concern in teaching writing to the slow learner. Speed is relatively unimportant as the slow learner will probably never have to produce any great volume of written material or have to write under the pressure of time. The methods used to teach writing to slow learners should be chosen on the basis of their suitability for each child, rather than on their attractiveness to the teacher. Manuscript writing is generally preferred with slow learners because it is similar to print, it is relatively immune to poor craftsmanship, and it is possible to form its characters with less rhythmic motor coordination than is required for cursive writing [Johnson, 48; McElravy, 193]. Some children will be able to develop skill with cursive writing as well, but the teacher should urge transfer only if the child's manuscript skills are satisfactory.

HOME AND FAMILY LIFE

The slow learner's intellectual differences may set him apart in school but, after leaving school, he generally takes his place unnoticed alongside brighter peers—working, raising a family, and generally becoming involved in activities that build and perpetuate communities. It is assumed that the general school activities discussed thus far will assist the slow learner to become an effective and contributing member of society. The special subject area of home and family life has a particularly important role to play in developing skills, habits, and attitudes essential to successful adult adjustment. Several years of home and family life instruction will not overcome a lifetime of home neglect, particularly if such instruction does not actively involve the student's family. However, the program can exert considerable influence on slow students if it is based in the reality of the child's environment and has been preceded by a curriculum that stresses the development of life adjustment skills.

Home and family life education for slow learners places emphasis on meeting learners at their individual functioning levels and helping them broaden their horizons. The Department of Home Economics of the National Education Association notes, "For effective work with slow learners the key words to remember are: direct, concrete, orderly, and exploratory" [Fernandez, 209]. Subject matter content will be quite similar to that given normal children. As usual, the topics stressed will vary from group to group, the variation being dictated by the students' home experiences. General attention will be given to adapting recipes, food preparation methods, and general homemaking procedures to lower academic skills. The course content will include development of a vocabulary based on terms used in shopping, cooking, cleaning, and other homemaking activities. Special attention will be given to words whose use and meaning are easily confused; for example, baste as in sewing as opposed to baste in cooking, the yoke of a dress as opposed to the yolk of an egg, and the waist of a pair of trousers as opposed to waste [Fernandez, 209]. One of the most difficult problems encountered with culturally deprived slow learners is how to plan a program that will not threaten their cultural identity and thus alienate them from the material being presented. The child who is accustomed to foods prepared at home from basic ingredients may find it hard to accept or, eventually, to afford recipes and meals that require the dried, frozen, and prepackaged foods that characterize middle class America. There is some question, too, of the value of instructing students only in the use of the latest electrical and mechanical worksavers when custom or lack of finances preclude the use of these devices in the child's home. Although the television set has become a necessary accoutrement for the poor, the washboard is still more common than the washing machine.

The teacher should plan a program around his knowledge of each child's eating habits, customs in dress and home furnishing, and other related matters. Slow students must be helped to expand their knowledge of patterns of social behavior, new customs, and the use of efficient home procedures and implements. This knowledge can be learned and later utilized if the students gradually become aware of the relationships between their familiar patterns and those that exist in the larger society. Slow students must have the opportunity to thoughtfully reject those ideas that do not fit their desired living pattern. They must also have the opportunity to experience these ideas before they decide to accept or reject them. Slow learning should not, in itself, be allowed to predetermine eventual cultural level.

Even casual observation of modern advertising and selling techniques reveals their orientation to the lowest level of understanding and their use of language that is ambiguous, confusing, and incomplete. While no reliable figures are available, it is probably safe to conclude that these techniques cause the greatest hardship among the slow learning group. Home and family life instruction should pay more than the usual attention to make slow students more aware of obvious and subtle consumer frauds or costly deceptions. Slow learners usually do not read well enough to ferret out information on product quality and reasonable financing. Accordingly, they should be taught how to obtain this information verbally without committing themselves to a sale. Slow students should receive instruction on how to redress their grievances against shoddy merchandise and how to submit their complaints to the appropriate community agencies.

The home and family life curriculum is the logical and often the most comfortable area in which to introduce the topic of sex education. Sex education for the slow learner has no special content that differentiates it from sex education programs planned for normal or bright students. The rate and type of instruction must conform to the child's ability to understand what is being presented; this ability is determined by his intelligence level and environmental experience. A basic foundation for a mature sexuality can be developed more readily if sex education is integrated into the total framework of instruction rather than dissected into its biological, social, medical, and public health aspects. The goal is the fostering of an awareness of sex as an integral part of personal and community life rather than as an isolated or unmentionable element of living. The realization of this goal is not especially easy in a society that exploits sex in the commercial media and emphasizes its sensational aspects. Such exploitation and emphasis, however, can exist only in an atmosphere of ignorance and apathy. The sensationalistic approach to sex is unlikely to disappear as long as the established institutions in society are unwilling to replace ignorance and apathy with well-planned, carefully taught programs of sex and family life education.

The usual recipients of home and family life instruction are girls. Boys, too, should be allowed to participate in those aspects of the program that would appear to have eventual value for them. Some high school programs provide special courses for slow learning boys in food services; other programs give special consumer education courses to both boys and girls. These and similar programs may lead directly to career placement. If formal course instruction cannot be made available, boys may be allowed to participate in appropriate home economics activities during club periods or in after-school programs.

INDUSTRIAL ARTS

The slow learner is often perceived as a student who is short on brains but very handy; consequently, he is seen as an ideal candidate for the junior and senior high school shop classes. This misconception results in bitter teachers and bewildered students. Industrial arts, however, can be a pleasant and profitable experience for slow learners if the program's goals are oriented to the student's abilities and needs. The industrial arts program is rather self-motivating since it brings into the school many elements of the "real" world, a world that the slow child has learned to value over that of the school's. This inherent advantage is frequently lost when the industrial arts curriculum becomes more academic than many academic subjects as the result of the teacher's desire to upgrade his program and his image in the school.

Industrial arts for slow learners should be activity oriented. Lessons should be planned so that tools and processes are introduced gradually and sequentially; preliminary static instruction should be held to a minimum; projects should reflect the interests and background of each student whenever possible, and they should be planned so that they may be completed in two or three class sessions. Intricate work requiring tedious finishing should be avoided; simple surface treatments are best for the slow student.

While industrial arts activities will help pupils build an idea of sequential work procedures, slow learners cannot be expected to generalize many other habits and attitudes from their shop activities. Good workmanship, neatness, cleanliness, and similar attributes should be taught in specific terms and made concrete by careful planning that includes opportunities for each pupil to evaluate his own work.

As in other subjects, the slow learner will need many experiences in using a specific spoken and written vocabulary. This vocabulary will include the names and functions of tools and materials commonly used in unskilled and semiskilled occupations.

The use of tools for home repairs should also be emphasized in the industrial arts program. Instruction should help the slow student understand the limits of home repairs that are dictated by factors of skill, safety, and local regulation. For example, replacing a household fuse is a legitimate activity, replacing a fuse in a factory is not; cleaning a household drain is quite acceptable, replacing black iron pipe with copper tubing is not. It is important to include a continuous emphasis on safety. Sample topics to be covered include industrial safety rules, emergency shop fire-fighting techniques, and emergency first aid.

The teacher should attempt to break each lesson or project into its component parts and analyze inter-relationships. Such analysis often suggests methods and approaches that can simplify instruction and reduce the margin for student error. This point is illustrated by the teacher who stained spindle-turning stock while it was in the square state. When the student no longer saw the stain as he turned the work on his lathe, he knew that roundness had been achieved. As this example implies, the slow learner can be trusted to perform various machine operations if he is held to the same criteria for operating power tools that are applied to other students—namely, dexterity, maturity, and common sense.

The industrial arts shop should allow students to experience a number of industrial processes and materials so that the teacher may assess the students' vocational interests and potential. It is not important that the slow learner know how to identify all the hardwoods of North America or know in detail how saws are made. It is important that he be taught to generalize about the economic system in which he lives and to recognize the contribution that he can make to this system.

Just as home economics instruction should be available for boys, industrial arts instruction should be provided for girls. They should know how to use basic tools and materials and how to make common household repairs.

Industrial arts for slow learners is not a time killer nor is it beneath the dignity of the industrial arts instructor. The subject matter is of extreme importance to boys and girls and should be taught so that it will be of maximum usefulness to them later in life.

MATHEMATICS

Rapid change is becoming a well-established characteristic of the modern school. This growth follows a long period during which the schools seemed intent on fossilizing instruction rather than energizing it. Nowhere is curriculum change more evident than in mathematics. The "new" mathematics is a reaction to traditional mathematics teaching methods that tended to promote rote learning over understanding, sought standardization rather than discovery, and placed a premium on a sequence of instruction that cannot be defended in terms of modern learning theory. The newness of the "new" mathematics is found in the freedom given to the learner to discover mathematical principles, the emphasis placed on the use of materials that allow for multisensory manipulation, and the earlier introduction of true mathematics into the curriculum. A particularly distinguishing feature of the "new" math is the content it draws from the new technology of computerization.

The "new" mathematics has seen its greatest popularization with college-bound students. Although its emphasis on manipulation and structure would appear to make it a logical learning tool for the slower child, no systematic study has been made of how it might best serve him—although a number of isolated attempts at application are being made [Potter and Mallory, 226; School Mathematics Study Group, 230; Woodby, 233]. The slow learner is still taught mathematics in terms of *where* he happens to be rather than in terms of *who* he is. Accordingly, the following discussion will not distinguish between new and old, but it will describe various techniques in current use and remind teachers to approach mathematics education experimentally. Fehr [215], in discussing the modern mathematics approach, indicates:

> All this mathematics is to be taught to all pupils, the slow learners as well as the fast. However, it must be adapted . . . and for slow learners this means the use of many practical concrete experiences before they can be expected to acquire the concepts.

The necessary mathematical readiness program for slow learners includes experiences paralleling those of reading readiness. The student must generalize about size, shape, weight, distance, and other visual-motor information. A basic understanding of time sequence and the nature of groupings is also necessary, and the student will learn these and other prerequisites to formal instruction through many real experiences that involve all of his sensory pathways. As a matter of course, the teacher will probably expose the entire class of young students to these experiences. In this process he must take particular care to give his slower students clues as to what they will see, hear, and touch. He must also make immediate assessment of what his slow students have gained from their experiences in terms of goals set mutually by pupil and teacher.

The teacher should not confuse rote or computational readiness with true mathematical readiness. The slow child can often add and subtract before he is ready to understand the processes involved or able to transfer these processes to actual problem situations. To assume that the child who knows his number facts is competent in mathematics is similar to assuming that the child who knows how to recite the alphabet is able to read. Actual learning in mathematics may be said to begin when the child can translate the known objects and symbols of his physical world into mathematical terms.

The slow learner in a primary level class will be exposed to a program that attempts to develop an understanding of numbers and explains their use in basic computation. Curriculum goals will include establishment of a carefully controlled mathematical vocabulary oriented toward allowing the child to express his growing knowledge of numbers. Whenever possible, the terms used should be drawn from the child's own language. Terms having similar meanings (subtract, take-away, minus) should not be applied interchangeably until the definitions and use of each term is well established.

If the young slow pupil resorts to learning crutches, such as counting on his fingers or using marks on his paper, these self-help aids should be studied carefully. Rather than looking at crutches as something to be tolerated and then eliminated, it is vital for the teacher to determine why the child uses a particular technique. Such determination may reveal problems in understanding or may provide clues to how a child develops his individual approach to learning.

The teacher may meet individual differences in the primary classroom by using materials that stress discovery and provide for instruction at various learning levels. Arithmetic kits containing several manipulative devices may be very useful. Adkins [211] suggests that Christmas card boxes be used as containers for paste sticks wrapped in bundles of ten. Cardboard circles, plastic autos, and similar materials are also suggested for use in developing basic concepts. For group work, Adkins advocates the use of large-sized samples of the same materials. A kit using purchased items of a more structured nature is suggested for class use by Berndt [213]. The kit includes an abacus, place value chart, and flannel board (with flannel numbers, various forms, and representative cutouts). The exploratory board is also mentioned by Berndt. This teacher-made device consists of a piece of pegboard and golf tees of assorted colors. Counting, place value, number sets, and other activities may be illustrated or explored on this board. Bridges [214] also suggests a number of teacher-made primary aids that would appear to assist the slow child through manipulative activity. A number box containing paper strips is used to teach the base ten concept, and short dowel lengths strung together are used for counting. Holinger [219] presents a case study in which a functional slow learner was helped to higher achievement through the use of various discovery materials. Poker chips helped establish sequence in counting. Once the sequence was established, it was applied to many real objects found in the immediate environment. Poker chips in various colors were used to build comparison groupings for teaching the concepts of more, less, and equal. The sequence moved from the concrete to the semiconcrete and finally to abstract problems. Holinger's approach may be seen as a model that can be applied to individual slow learners in a regular classroom.

The consolidation of these rather isolated approaches into a total learning environment is possible through the use of the elementary mathematics laboratory. Rasmussen [228] defines the mathematics laboratory as follows:

To the child it is a playroom where things can be counted, moved, re-arranged, stacked, packed, wrapped, measured, joined, partitioned. It is a room with things to be weighed and weighing instruments, machines with buttons, levers, and cranks that count, record, and project; with books for browsing, books for reading, and empty books to be written into; with objects of interesting shapes and many sizes to be used for building and comparing.

To the teacher it is a planned environment in which one puts children, so that each question one poses to them about numbers or shapes can be illustrated in innumerable ways. It is a room in which the children can have the best possible support for problem-solving through concrete experiences and readily available tools, and where they can verify through experiments the correctness of their answers independently of the teacher.

In this laboratory environment the teacher can build readiness and continue to develop the child's mathematical ability. Such a laboratory may be incorporated into a regular classroom, but, ideally is a separate room with special features and equipment that allows attention to individual differences. Such a room could be justified in terms of its general advantages to all children in addition to its special advantages for the slow learner and the culturally deprived.

The intermediate level slow learner requires an increasingly specialized program of mathematics instruction. Manipulative materials lose their usefulness since they are considered babyish. Standard texts do not maintain interest because of high reading and abstraction levels. Yet, fundamental number skills still must be mastered, and additional practice must be given in applied topics (using money, telling time, measuring).

One method of adjusting the intermediate mathematics curriculum to all learners is to plan units that provide experience in a wide range of number skills. Typical units center around a class visit to a cafeteria, a class party, buying Christmas gifts from a catalogue, class craft projects, and class trips (real and imaginary) to local and distant places. The teacher may help students generate their own study materials through discussions based on these experiences. If duplicated sheets are prepared by the class, they may be compiled, along with commercially prepared duplicated sheets and pages selected from workbooks, into individually tailored texts.

The teacher of a heterogeneous group should not succumb to the lure of dividing mathematics into pure and applied forms with the intention of giving the former to the bright and the latter to the slow. While interest and motivation can be derived from problems that deal with actual situations in the child's life, the problem-solving process is dependent upon somewhat abstract, somewhat non-life-related mathematical principles that must receive equal attention. Accordingly, a practical math program that ignores fundamentals will be of little benefit to any child.

The teacher of slow learners in junior and senior high school will extend the mathematical experiences of the intermediate grades; he will also introduce the pupil to a program of specific mathematical preparation for adult living. This preparation should provide the student with the ability to communicate mathematically in a technologically oriented society, and it should assure his competence in the traditional skills of "supermarket" arithmetic. Greenholz [216] describes an experimental program that introduces the slow learner to a number of mathematical concepts including the set theory, mathematical patterns, the number line, and operations with whole and rational numbers. The emphasis is on instruction suited to the slow child's characteristics, the use of methods that simplify computation, and the utilization of discovery techniques. A similar project is described by Lerch [224]. This program is planned for seventh-grade students; its main organizational features are grouping slow learners in self-contained classes and assigning teachers to slow pupils for the entire day. The plan of instruction utilizes a topical approach, each topic being sustained for two to four weeks. Interclass groupings are used to adjust the program content to individual ability levels. Diagnostic tests and content inventories are used to determine groups. The present results indicate that the experimental program is more effective for low achieving students than is a traditional program.

Adler [212] indicates that the secondary school program should help the student, through an exploration of basic mathematical laws and the use of mathematical experiments, to maintain and relearn those concepts introduced earlier. Similar programming is suggested by Sobel [231]. He feels that proper reteaching should capitalize on the added maturity that the student has gained through chronological growth. Such growth may bring within his grasp many of the processes that caused him earlier difficulties. To facilitate reteaching, motivation may be achieved and a sense of failure avoided by introducing slow students to "the side roads" of mathematics. These side roads are said to include various systems of numeration, ancient methods of computation, and elementary surveying. A study by Krulik [223] indicates that if the teacher emphasizes meaning and builds appreciation he can help slow learners achieve in mathematical areas that are usually considered beyond them. He reports on the specific areas of coordinate geometry and elementary statistics.

A number of authors suggest the use of concrete materials and experiences as effective practices for teaching mathematics in the secondary school. Krulik [222] describes the use of dice and pennies to teach the idea of central tendency. The class conducted by Kovinow [221] established its own insurance company. Students paid small sums to the company, and it invested the money through rentals, sales, and loans. Payments were made to students for various claims. The entire class kept careful records and participated in closing the monthly books. Parrish [225] describes a classroom that looks like a "mathematics room." The desk is painted to simulate a cubic yard, and many manipulative materials and student-made charts are available for use. In this mathematics room various games are used to stimulate learning. Proctor [227] has each child keep his own mathematics kit that includes materials useful for studying whole-number and decimal fractions. She makes extensive use of the bulletin board where a class-constructed number line is displayed. Games similar to Bingo and Whist are played to reinforce number facts. A program for retarded and slow learning pupils that makes extensive use of graphs is described by Willerding [232]. Students construct simple bar graphs showing their own weights, ages, and number of children in their families. Willerding feels that graphing is an effective way of teaching about relationships between people and objects and is very useful in explaining the idea of averages. Greenholz [216] suggests that the concreteness essential to the solution of verbal problems be obtained through breaking the problem content into small repetitive steps and using a number of questions that require generalization and synthesis. In building the ability to use various mathematical definitions, Greenholtz indicates that the understanding expressed by the student is much more important than the language used. Jacobs, Bollenbacher, and Keiffer [220] report on the use of modern media to teach mathematics. They used television to teach a course in seventh-grade mathematics to students who were one and one-half to two and one-half years retarded in arithmetic achievement. Two classes were used for the experimental instruction. Two other classes served as controls. After a seven month period, it was concluded that televised instruction was no more effective than regular instruction in teaching seventh-grade mathematics to pupils who show low achievement. This report notwithstanding, the new technology is being used increasingly to teach slow learners mathematics.

Multisensory aids and new media often add a dimension to provide insight for the low achiever that he does not get from chalkboard or the printed page. For example, the overhead projector furnished avenues to capture the attention and curiosity of the learner. Student-made transparencies are an asset, for they challenge the learner to organize his ideas; furthermore, this technique gives recognition to the low achiever for his accomplishment. [Woodby, 233]

Desk calculators, electric or manual, are being used to allow slow students to check problems first worked by hand. The machines apparently provide motivation to students who see mathematics as a failure activity. The devices also serve as a reassurance to students who have poor computational skills, and they make it possible to test the understanding of a process aside from the computation involved [Groenendyk, 217]. Available information indicates that the slow student actually improves hand computation skills when using a calculator. The gain in skill seemingly relates to the fact that the machine removes the fear of failure and provides the structure through which computation processes may be understood more clearly.

Flow charting, a concept borrowed from computer programming, is also being used to teach mathematics to slow learners in the secondary school. A flow chart is a way of writing down all of the steps involved in a particular process. The concept of flow charting consists of asking a series of questions. As each question is written, it is answered yes or no. The result of each yes or no is recorded in an appropriate box. The idea recorded may be an additional question or a descriptive instruction that leads to further questioning. Each response provides a further link to the eventual solution of the problem. An example of a simple flow chart as adapted from Groenendyk [218] is given below.

Flow charting allows a student to see his thinking in a concrete form and permits him to raise questions about the steps he has taken and the steps he plans to take. There is no correct way of making a flow chart; consequently, there is a reduction in the feeling of failure that arises when the slow student compares his work to that of other students. Flow charting indicates how the child thinks as well as how much content he has mastered, but it can become tiresome unless it is based on problems having high intrinsic interest and is not made the primary teaching method. With these cautions in mind, teachers will find that flow charting offers exciting possibilities for introducing mathematical ideas to slow learners.

The mathematics laboratory is also considered to be a very useful tool for teaching secondary level slow learners. Although elementary school mathematics laboratories are not very prevalent, it appears that a high proportion of secondary schools employ some type of mathematics laboratory. This laboratory is usually conducted by a mathematics specialist and includes many devices useful in teaching

ERROR IN MEASUREMENT

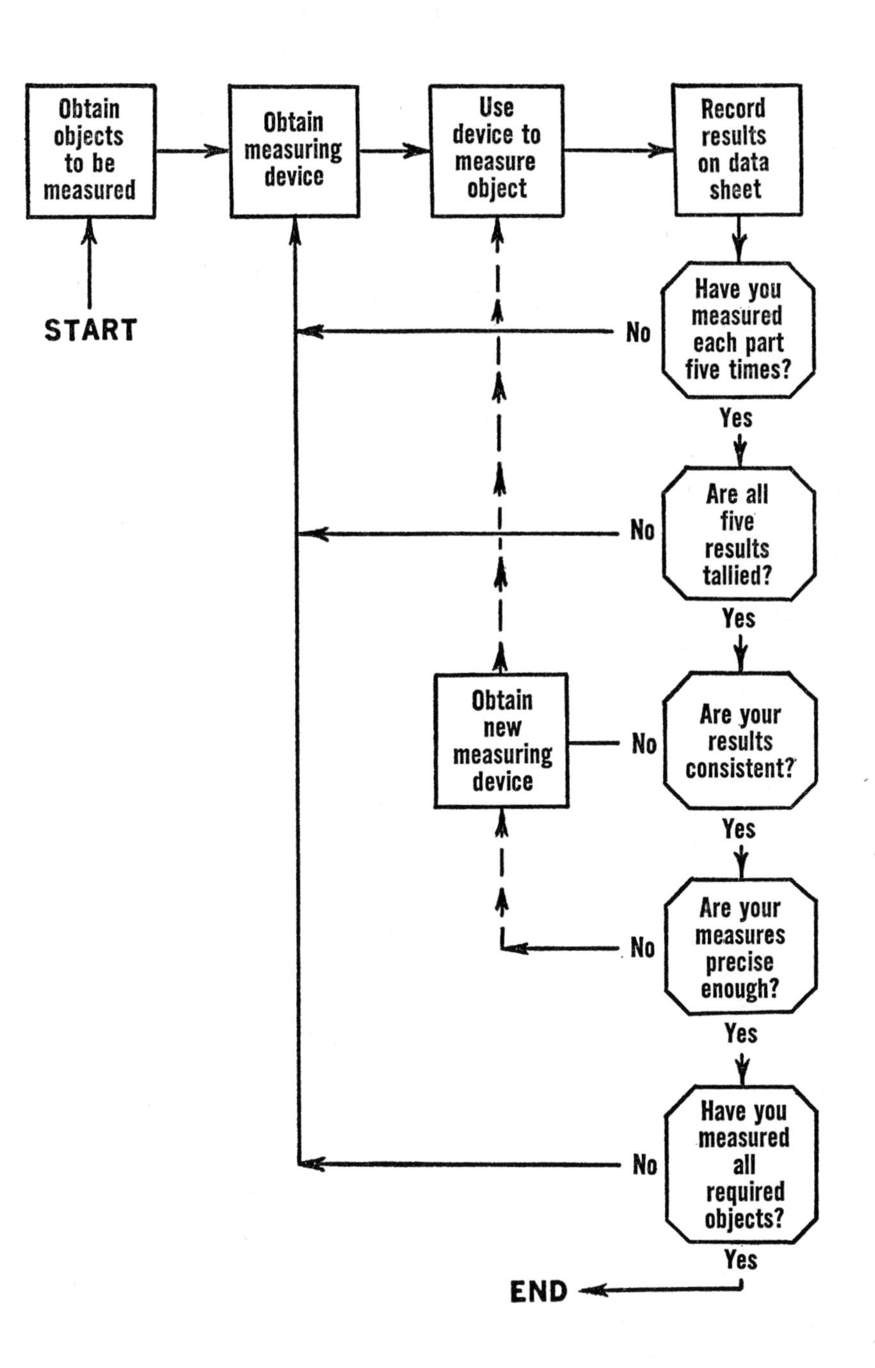

advanced mathematical concepts. Items of particular interest to programs for slow learners include the desk calculator, overhead projector, steel tape measure, still camera, stop watch, opaque projector, transit, pantograph, tape recorder, plainimeter, various models of mathematics concepts, common measuring devices, geometric figures, and familiar objects having mathematical stimulus [Potter and Mallory, 226; Groenendyk, 218].

A review of the social, psychological, and learning problems relating to low mathematics achievement is included in the C.A.M.P. conference report [Rosenbloom, 229]. The report also includes a brief description of experimental programs in Los Angeles, Detroit, Fort Worth, Baton Rouge, and Wynne, Arkansas.

Teachers are encouraged to use the latest methods, but, ultimately, mathematics instruction for slow learners is more dependent upon good teaching than special tricks or unusual devices. The child's developmental level must be known, and his program should be planned in terms of the experiences brought to the classroom. The slow learner in mathematics has an early awareness of his slowness but does not equate slowness with failure until the teacher communicates this feeling. Most teachers are concerned with content quantity. The key to teaching slow learners is content quality. The subject interdependency of mathematics must receive constant attention. Mathematics should be taught with emphasis on its natural correlation to reading, spelling, verbal expression, social studies, and other curriculum topics. Mathematics is constantly changing, and many mathematical ideas—once considered extremely esoteric—have become necessary and familiar supports for a burgeoning technology. The mathematics curriculum must also change and must include those students who were formerly considered mathematically educated upon achieving competency in basic arithmetical skills. All through the school years, the slow student's ability to explore must be extended, and his facility to abstract should be increased. The newer technology and its newer mathematics offer solutions as well as challenges.

MUSIC EDUCATION

Although it is said that "music hath charms to soothe a savage breast," music education has had some difficulty charming or otherwise establishing itself a position in the school curriculum as a legitimate subject, and it still may be considered an educational frill. When some apparently strong music programs are looked at carefully, they appear to gain their strength by fulfilling specialized needs—that is, a sports-supporting band or a prize-winning chorus—rather than by offering every student an additional opportunity for personal enrichment. Because music apparently has not attained full curriculum equality with other subjects—and research thereby suffers—little is known about what constitutes an effective program for those children who exhibit negative differences in vocal control, aural understanding, and other musical characteristics and competencies [Petzold, 236].

General suggestions for assisting the handicapped student to fit into regular music classes include the use of a number of creative activities that allow the child to experiment and explore [Sur and Schuller, 237]. Nye [235] indicates that poor responses may be modified by finding their cause, and he states:

> Music is particularly well suited to provide for these differences because of the great variety of activities possible through which the different ability levels can be accommodated.

Activities that appear most suitable for slow learners are those that involve students physically and draw upon the musical resources present in their environment. There is no special musical curriculum for slow learners, but there are a number of specific activities that will help make music a vital experience rather than a distasteful one.

Popular music can provide the basis for introducing music to slow learners because it represents the familiar and thus signifies security. Many students can participate actively in the popular music phase by bringing their own records to school. Popular music has its roots in other kinds of music, and these roots—more formal or more informal—may be traced by listening to records, singing representative songs, and making and playing appropriate instruments. Student-made instruments are most effective in illustrating various rhythmic patterns and in analyzing various styles of musical expression. Early school experiences with rhythm instruments, and later instruction on simple flutes or similar instruments, can help slow learners develop an interest and confidence in performing on standard musical instruments. The teacher's study of the slow child's neighborhood will reveal use of the guitar or other instruments that may also be the source of music in school; this study may also reveal some unorthodox methods of teaching and learning music that, though pedagogically somewhat unacceptable, may still be rather effective. Music as movement may be explored through a program of dance instruction. Simple dances or movements to music may be used with younger children, while social dancing may be a very important part of the curriculum for the older students. Many opportunities should be provided the slow learner to expand his musical background through attending musical performances of various kinds. Intensive preparation and follow-up activities should accompany such experiences. These activities might include an explanation of what is to be seen, comparisons of one performance with others, decisions as to what to look for, and discussions of how music can be appreciated in several different ways. Although more abstract than most of the activities previously described, musical history should not be ignored, particularly when it can be related to the students' interests or ethnic and cultural background. Historical studies provide many opportunities for students to make models, dioramas, and other constructions that allow physical expression. The study of notation and formal musical symbols is not beyond the slow learner's comprehension and, in fact, may hold considerable interest for him if he is first given a strong reason for his study by being exposed to a variety of musical experiences.

The discipline problems and disinterest that may be evidenced in the music class are more often than not an expression of poor teaching ability rather than poor learning ability. The music teacher or the classroom teacher will find music to be a most rewarding subject for slow learners, if the student is given an opportunity to find his place in music. This concept does not by any means imply complete musical freedom or the lack of any formal instruction. The concept demands a structure that is tight enough to be quite flexible, for only in musical security is musical diversity possible.

PHYSICAL EDUCATION

Slow learners have the ability to achieve at or very close to normal levels in most physical education activities. Slow learning, in itself, does not imply any reduction in physical functioning. The poor environmental conditions often associated with slow learning may deny some students the proper diet required for good physical conditioning. Poor environmental conditions also lead to a high incidence of infectious diseases and often imply substandard medical care. Therefore, it is possible that slow learners will have secondary handicaps that must be considered when the physical education program is planned.

It is extremely important for the physical education teacher to consider the failure syndrome that the slow learner transfers from other school activities. Despite obvious athletic potential, he may be unwilling to test his capabilities because of past disappointments. Since the slow learner loses the protection of his class group when engaging in team activities, he may be particularly reticent to participate in extracurricular sports. Despite these cautious words, many slow learners are successful in physical education, particularly when the teacher has helped the student systematically to build his confidence. Physical education, of itself, can work no miracles, but it may provide the structure through which a thoughtful teacher can achieve significant accomplishments.

The physical education program for slow learners may include more emphasis on corrective exercise than is usual, will give extra attention to building good habits of general health and personal hygiene, and should stress leisure time activities appropriate to the slow child's environment. Particular attention should be given to helping students discover, develop, and use community recreation facilities. An effort should also be made to correlate physical education instruction with the student's other school work. In other respects, the physical education program will parallel that given to all other pupils.

SCIENCE

For most of its history, the American school has treated science as a disparate subject studied only in high school. Recently, a burgeoning technology touching on every aspect of life has wrought a significant change in the school's science curriculum. The study of topics drawn from a number of scientific fields is now begun routinely in the kindergarten and woven with increasing complexity into almost all subject matter throughout the elementary and secondary school. The slow learner will, as a matter of course, be exposed to the newer emphasis on science in the curriculum and must be helped to understand and apply those elements that will benefit him. He must be shown his place in science. This place probably will not involve creation. It most certainly will involve consumption and may include decision making through the use of the adult's voting rights.

There is no need to formulate special scientific subject matter for the slow learner. There is definite need to stimulate his curiosity and clarify his understanding of his natural, synthetic, and mechanical surroundings. The common complaint that the slow child lacks imagination, inventiveness, and curiosity in science is in part true, and these characteristics can be attributed to his deficient powers of abstraction and reasoning. The transition of these weaknesses into major learning handicaps, however, usually results from teaching methods that stress conformity rather than creativity, passiveness rather than curiosity, and repetition rather than imagination. Science for the slow learner should be an accumulation of discoveries rather than an accumulation of facts. It should encompass the following:

1. Allow the learner to be at least minimally conversant in scientific matters, particularly those that interest his peers.
2. Allow the learner to follow up scientific interests stimulated by television and other mass media so that he may achieve a basic understanding of the principles being discussed.
3. Prepare the learner to understand and use the scientific content he will require as an adult.
4. Allow the learner to perceive the relationship between the levels of scientific knowledge required for a realistic vocational choice.
5. Allow the learner to explain natural phenomena in his environment that may give rise to superstition or unnecessary concern.
6. Allow the learner to discover the rewards of intellectual inquiry and establish the practice of such inquiry as an important element in his life.
7. Prepare the learner to use scientific knowledge in making judgments about economic consumption and living conditions.

One of the teaching themes stressed repeatedly here and in all literature on teaching the slow learner is the principle of pupil involvement. The slow child learns best when he comes into direct contact with the subject matter and assumes a role in organizing the learning approach and sequence. Science is particularly suited to this theme. When the child begins to wonder how things grow, he can plant a flower bulb, water it, and watch it grow—or he can fail to water it and watch it die. He can plant beans in soil pressed between two sheets of glass and observe the growth of roots. He can initiate many similar activities that answer his inquiries while giving him additional questions to ponder. Throughout his school experience, every child should have access to the world laboratory that surrounds him and should be encouraged to experiment and learn from what he sees.

For the teacher who envisions chaos as the logical extension of the suggestions made above, it should be added that science instruction has an inherent structure and order. This characteristic matches the slow learner's need for step-by-step instruction and inter-relatedness of subject topics. It also provides considerable assistance in curriculum planning. One laboratory experience tends to stimulate another and to suggest correlations with mathematics, social studies, and other subject areas.

Laboratory experiences do not constitute the entire fabric of science instruction. The child's environment, the mass media, and science texts constitute other sources of scientific questions and answers. The slow learner's reading problem may limit his use of text materials, particularly in the upper grades. This should pose no major problem, as popular treatments of science content are available in rather readable form in current magazines and newspapers. They are usually accompanied by extensive pictorial material that texts rarely provide.

In the primary years, the science curriculum places emphasis on the child's natural surroundings. As the class enters into a discussion of various topics, the slower children should be given special help to overcome fears resulting from ignorance or misinformation: the moon is not about to fall from the sky, black cats are no more unlucky than other kinds, and the real danger of walking under a ladder is that someone may drop something onto your head. The children should be helped also to recognize problems in their environment that they may avoid or correct: old buildings are not good playgrounds because there are many things that can cut, or fall, or collapse to hurt you; rats don't come because they like people but because they like what people throw away; electricity can be very helpful but must be put to work in special ways and cannot be seen or touched like water or other home helpers. Young children have a natural curiosity about how things work. The classroom should include a collection of toys and other objects that invite questions and manipulation. Small animals and other growing things also are a necessary part of the classroom environment. There is a particular value in having all children care for and make regular verbal or written reports on their observations of classroom plants and animals.

The intermediate grades are the time in which field visits are particularly profitable. The children now have sufficient language facility to question and report on what they see. Science books also become more important as language is developed. The older children are somewhat more capable of making changes in poor environmental conditions that are recognized by scientific inquiry, and these children can be organized into reporting or clean-up teams. Scientific topics will be drawn increasingly from the study of other subject matter, as the curriculum broadens from its earlier emphasis on fundamental skill development.

The junior and senior high schools provide time in which earlier instruction can be expanded and enriched—particularly if science is considered a subject that permeates the curriculum [Rudman, 242]. In the many schools where the traditional subject matter organization is followed, science may lose much of its earlier attractiveness and become a tedium. This is true primarily because traditional organization implies heavy emphasis on the use of texts that are beyond the slow student's reading ability, the memorization of facts that have little meaning to him, and the introduction to technical processes that are beyond his powers of comprehension. When the slow learner is placed in regular subject matter classes, the secondary school teacher's first alternative is to hope that interest will be maintained through content dilution. The science teacher also may elect to rewrite parts of the standard text to reduce vocabulary problems. To assist this effort, Moore [241] lists vocabulary guides and readability formulas. This approach is often less than successful because the original science content may be too abstract for slow students or because reading material preparation requires considerable skill, experience, and time. Lichtenstein [239] describes an experience in a regular biology class where considerable attention was given to building reading skills. Lichtenstein reports that the experience resulted in substantial improvement in reading ability, but there is no indication of how much biology was taught. One of the few large-scale projects to develop special science subject matter materials for slow learners is that of the Biological Sciences Curriculum Study [Liebherr and Peterson, 240]. A special materials committee has prepared a comprehensive guide for biology teachers who work with slow learners. The primary goal of the booklet is to help prepare teachers to meet the challenge of the "academically unsuccessful student" through the careful use of special project materials. These materials are designed for grade ten; their approach places great emphasis on laboratory work and the understanding of inquiry. Suggestions for using the materials with slow students stress matching content to characteristics; it is also suggested that a sharp distinction be made between inherent intellectual traits and those that appear as the result of poor instruction. The guide gives equal attention to teacher and student, and it attempts to help the former feel comfortable with unfamiliar approaches. Suggested teaching methods rely on open-ended activities, flexibility, careful sequencing, and careful review of student progress.

Ennis [238] describes a physics course that allows slow students to make practical applications of various subject topics. Physics rules and principles are stated by students after the projects' completion. The attractive, useful products resulting from the class experiences help maintain student interest. The program was plagued, however, by the high costs, the teachers' reluctance to experiment, and the need for extensive preparation time. A solution to the first problem would now seem possible through an application for federal or private funds. The latter problems, however, seem little reduced by the passage of time.

Over-all, it appears that the slow learner in secondary school will continue to be handicapped in science instruction until such time as the science curriculum is reorganized to reflect the characteristics that favor the slow learner in the science curriculum of the elementary school.

Science instruction can be most profitable for the slow learner at all levels if it embodies freedom for the student to explore, ready accessibility of the teacher to stimulate questions and provide means by which answers can be found, constant attention to environmental stimuli, and use of all available scientific resources—whether they be formal texts or the televising of a journey into space. Science is born out of creativity, and it is only logical that it be taught in a creative way to all learners.

SOCIAL STUDIES

Many basic concepts underlie the subject specialty identified as "social studies." These concepts include an appreciation of the national heritage and an understanding of the operation of local, state, and national governments. They encompass the responsibilities and rewards of citizenship, a realization of the economic importance of local and national industrial systems, and an awareness of regional differences in persons, places, and things. These and similar concepts are of vital importance to the slow learner, yet they are difficult to teach because of their abstractness and their traditional reliance on static instructional methodologies.

The laboratory approach that characterizes science instruction for slow learners is also very appropriate when applied to the social studies. Like all children, the slow learner will benefit from a carefully planned exposure to his social environment, particularly since this approach can be effected without instituting the special grouping that suggests slowness. The laboratory approach will involve all community resources and, thus, will set the stage for a continuous relationship between the learner and the agencies and services he may use in adulthood.

Subject content in social studies will be most effective if presented to stimulate gradual movement from the immediate and concrete to the remote and abstract. The basic structure begins with the child and moves sequentially to his family, to his neighborhood, to the city, to the county, to the state, to the region, to the nation, to the continent, to the hemisphere, to the world, to the universe, and possibly beyond. The structure should also provide for a study of the changes in relationships that occur between the maturing student and the various elements of his social environment.

The primary teacher must give particular attention to helping the slow child identify himself in relation to others in the classroom. His intellectual immaturity may be reflected in inappropriate social behavior. If the teacher does not help the child understand and overcome this behavior, it may result in early peer rejection and continued immaturity. The social studies topics of the primary grades are generally appropriate for slow learners. Care must be taken to ensure that students integrate various experiences and develop their abstractive powers. Slow learning often implies cultural difference, and teachers must consider the extent and range of these differences if their social studies content is to be within the experience grasp of slow students. Visits to various neighborhoods, group discussions, and other activities should be planned so that differences are not hardened into prejudices.

By the time he reaches adulthood, the slow learner often harbors feelings of bitterness and resentment born of the realization that his vocational choices are limited. From his earliest school years, the child should be helped to avoid this disappointment. Through exposure to a number of community occupations, he should be helped to grow from the phantasy stage of vocational development to a stage in which he is able to match his known abilities against his vocational observations. Such development is a subtle process. It must be accomplished without predetermining the child's future or involving him prematurely in the vocational selection process.

In the intermediate years, the slow learner will begin to expand his knowledge of society to reach beyond his immediate neighborhood and to spend more school time learning social studies from books and other formal materials. To be successful, intermediate social studies instruction must recognize the growing learning gap between slow and nonslow learners. The slow learner continues to require extensive field experience. He will learn some facts from simplified texts, but he will learn most effectively by building models and dioramas, participating in dramatic sketches, and recreating scenes of the past and wonders of the present by paint rather than by pen. In heterogeneous groups, differentiation of instruction may be accomplished best by use of the project or unit method. This approach allows students to work on various parts of an over-all learning sequence according to their interests and ability. A work corner set aside for construction related to social studies can provide an outlet for the slower student. Slow students may find it easier to study social problems in the community if the teacher organizes small study groups that are balanced in ability. Or, slow students may interview and discuss while brighter students read and write. Whatever techniques are decided upon, their use should be continued for long periods of time.

The junior and senior high school years provide slow learners with additional opportunities for exploring their social environment. They should receive specific preparation for assuming the duties of a worker and a citizen. Earlier observations of the community and its workers should be updated through well-planned field study and class discussion. Particular attention should be given to community agencies that may assist the student or his family now or in the future. Many agencies are not used, or are misused, because people have no understanding of them or have little contact with them until a time of crisis. The slow student's proneness to failure and his method of handling this failure are other important areas of teacher concern. Building healthy boy-girl social relationships should also be part of the curriculum.

In the secondary school, the mass media provide an important adjunct to the traditional subject content. The use of various media must, of course, be accompanied by a careful evaluation. For example, when D'Ambrosio [245] suggests that news clippings be used to stimulate class discussion, he raises the problem of selecting items that can logically be considered of educational value. Koob [251] assumes that editorials usually contain some ideas of substance and proposes their use in teaching social studies and English. Editorials would be selected by the teacher, mimeographed, read in class, and discussed. Herman [248] questions the use of newspaper articles with poor readers and suggests the substitution of political cartoons.

The activity method appears to be especially popular at the secondary level. Koch [249] recommends the use of active discussion that evolves from actual experiences. Peller [254] reports the use of early American history units that include the construction of period objects that are contrasted to modern objects. Switzer [255] gains involvement by having students in world geography participate in a number of field experiences, find simple references, and correct their own tests. D'Ambrosio [245] approaches history by having students pretend they are reporters covering historical events.

Social studies is important for slow learners. Teaching must stress personal and social adjustment and include many opportunities for student involvement. The slow learner can learn if social studies instruction begins at his social level and assumes that he can become a contributing member of his society.

An interesting sidelight to the discussion on adapting social studies for slow learners is that there is a growing movement to suggest similar adaptations for all learners. The traditional, factual method of teaching is being questioned and a "new" social studies is evolving that parallels the "new" math and the "new" science [Fenton, 246]. The number of facts available have far outgrown the teacher's ability to impart them, and the teaching of facts clearly does not prepare the individual to meet the ever-changing social demands of his environment. The trend in teaching social studies to nonslow learners at the secondary level appears to be toward greater involvement of the student in the learning process, more emphasis on drawing the instructional materials and content from his immediate surroundings, and greater concern with activities that encourage learning through exploration. The proponents of the "new" social studies apparently have had little time to consider the slow learner, and no accurate assessment can be made of his reaction to newer emphases. While it appears that the slow learner may profit from the new program's focus on involvement, there is danger that the slow student may become confused unless he is carefully led across the leaps in inductive thinking that the evolving teaching methods appear to demand.

One project that illustrates the "new" social studies approach is the High School Geography Project of the Association of American Geographers. This project attempts to develop a curriculum that provides students with information and understandings of use to them throughout their lives [Kohn, 250]. This project, like several of its counterparts in the physical and social sciences, is not designed for slow learners. However, the expressed philosophy and methodology may make it much easier and more natural for the subject matter specialist to work effectively with slow learners. As Helburn [247] indicates:

> Geographers are, therefore, taking searching looks in two directions: at the nature of education and at the nature of geography. Scientists and educators are finding that what a child should be taught and how he should be taught are inextricably intertwined. Subject matter cannot be divorced from method, nor the logic of the subject from the psychologic of teaching.

SUMMARY OF SPECIFIC ADAPTATIONS

The preceding review of adaptations in specific school subjects is based on a number of assumptions. These relate to how the slow learner learns and how subject matter should be integrated into a total concept of curriculum organization. Attention to individual subject adaptations must stress the need for pupil involvement that can be encouraged through the use of familiar learning clues. Other points to consider in making adaptations are: the teacher must be aware of any unique problems that slow learning may interpose between the subject matter and the learner; the subject matter must be viewed in terms of its importance to the learner, not in terms of its place in the traditional educational hierarchy; the basic excitement and creative elements of the subject matter must be preserved, even though new approaches are employed.

In addition to considering specific adaptations in individual subject areas, teachers should also be aware of several over-all approaches that are applicable to most subject matter fields. Several of these general approaches are described in the pages that follow.

AUDIOVISUAL MATERIALS

One of the most common attributes ascribed to audiovisual materials is their effectiveness with slow learners. The assumption is based on the fact that audiovisual materials are generally novel and therefore less threatening. Also, they provide instructional reinforcement by simultaneous stimulation of several sensory pathways.

Audiovisual techniques and materials can be very useful in motivating and stimulating slow learners, and in imparting information to them. However, the effectiveness of audiovisual instruction lies not in the techniques or materials themselves, but in the introduction, application, and evaluation of an imaginative teacher. Contrary to popular opinion, the thoughtful use of audiovisual instruction takes more time and effort than the use of more traditional materials, and this is probably one reason why so little effective audiovisual instruction is used with normal or slow learners.

The same general rules for using audiovisual materials with regular learners may be applied to the slower student. The audiovisual materials selected must be chosen for some particular instructional value of their own that cannot be duplicated by the use of less expensive, less time-consuming, or potentially more effective materials or techniques. The teacher must select an emphasis that he expects the material to achieve; this emphasis may be on the introduction of new material, expansion of an idea presented previously, review of content that was taught some time ago, pictorial illustration of an idea originally approached through reading, auditory reinforcement of material that had been presented visually, testing of previously taught material, or other emphases that may occur to the teacher. The presentation should be confined to one emphasis at a time, and the teacher must be familiar with each material before it is used. Otherwise, he cannot claim to be using the material for any particular value or emphasis. The teacher's preview knowledge should be incorporated into activities planned to introduce students to the material. From their introductory activities, students should gain an over-all picture of the material's content, an idea of any manipulation or involvement they are expected to provide, the specific points they should look for, and any post-presentation activity they may expect. Follow-up activities should be planned as carefully as those that precede the presentation.

If the teacher follows basic cautions in planning the use of audiovisual materials, he can ensure at least minimal success. To improve his rate of success with slow learners, the teacher should also observe the following guides.

Instructional aids that stimulate concrete thinking and direct involvement in an idea or activity may be used for introductory purposes or as the prime teaching medium. More abstract approaches should be reserved for review, reinforcement, expansion, or testing of subject matter that has been introduced concretely.

Speed of presentation is sometimes a problem with the slow learner, particularly with motion pictures. The problem may be reduced by showing a film through once, then showing again with stops for emphasis on main points. This procedure is most effective with equipment that allows exposure of single frames. Otherwise, the process of turning on lights for questioning may be distracting, while the discussion of main points in total darkness may be disastrous.

Some audiovisual materials provide slow learners with more distraction than instruction. The teacher must lend considerable assistance to the student if he is to develop an ability to sort important ideas from the novelty, stimulation, and excitement that the material employs for motivation. The fact that the slow learner is interested in a material and appears to be enjoying it doesn't ensure that he is learning anything. His general inability to learn from incidental clues carries over to audiovisual instruction and must be compensated for through introductory and follow-up activities.

The teacher should recognize the role that slow learners may play in maintaining and presenting audiovisual materials. Many slow students, with proper instruction, can learn to set up and operate various pieces of audiovisual equipment and can perform simple repairs to films, slide mounts, record-case binding, and other items.

Pictures for Learning. Some of the most available visual materials are printed illustrations. These pictures may be cut from magazines, travel folders, calendars, and similar sources, and they may be used for language development activities, for bulletin board displays, for stimulating artistic expression, for reinforcing points made in discussion periods, and for other teaching purposes. Each picture should be mounted on construction paper or similar backing. Consistent use of the 8½ by 11-inch size will permit easy filing. Each picture should be coded with the proper letter designation. As pictures are added they should receive consecutive numbering. The code and number in print approximately one inch high should be placed on the back of the picture mount in the upper right-hand corner. Each picture category should be placed in a separate file folder with the category code clearly marked. A classification system helpful in setting up a picture file may be developed around topics commonly found in curriculum guides from grades 1 to 6.

Bulletin Boards. Bulletin boards and other classroom displays often provide visual stimuli for learning. The teacher who is interested in improving his bulletin boards may gain some ideas from the following publications:

Koskey, Thomas A. *Baited Bulletin Boards,* San Francisco: Fearon Publishers, 1954.

Koskey, Thomas A. *Bulletin Board Idea Sources,* San Francisco: Fearon Publishers, 1963.

Weseloh, Anne R. D. *E-Z Bulletin Boards,* San Francisco: Fearon Publishers, 1959.

Lettering Systems. One of the most difficult tasks in preparing visual displays is providing lettering that is well proportioned, attractive, legible, and quick to prepare. A number of lettering aids are available that make this task easier.

Cardboard letters are one of the cheapest and most convenient of the reusable letter systems. The letters are die cut of heavy cardboard. Usually, only block letters are available, but they come in several sizes. Letters may be glued to a background with rubber cement, or they can be attached with pins. Cardboard letters are very useful for bulletin boards and can be traced for writing practice. They are available from most school supply houses; price depends on letter size. The Mutual Aids Company, 1946 Hillburst Avenue, Los Angeles, California, carries a large line of cardboard letters in many sizes and eight colors.

The chart marker is one of the oldest of the school sign systems. It consists of a set of rubber type letters that are inked on a stamp pad. The letters are held in a wooden or metal holder. The system is available in several type faces and sizes. Initial cost is moderate and continued use is inexpensive, but it is difficult to obtain an even impression and to maintain a straight line. Sets are usually available from school supply or office supply concerns.

Sets of flannel or felt letters are particularly useful on a flannel board, and, if pinned, can add considerable color to a bulletin board. These letters are large and readily seen; they are rather expensive and should be used over again. They do tend to fad in the sunlight, and their tendency to stretch makes them appear untidy when pinned for extensive periods. School supply firms stock felt letters. A specific source of wool and cotton felt letters is the Visual Specialties Company, 5701 West Vernor, Detroit, Michigan.

Plastic letters are available in several sizes in either pin backs or for use with a special adhesive. The pin backs are re-usable. Letters are available in gold, silver, and six colors, and they are relatively expensive. One source is Sye Gorman Company, 18431 James Couzens Highway, Detroit, Michigan.

Pressure-sensitive letters are a very versatile and simple system. The letters are not re-usable. They come on a sheet that is placed over the material to be marked and rubbed with a flat surface. The desired letter is thus transferred to the sign or poster being made. The letters are fairly permanent. They are available in over fifteen type faces in upper and lower case. Five colors are available. Each sheet carries a complete font. Although rather expensive, these letters are extremely useful for signs and permanent bulletins. They are carried by Arthur Brown & Brothers, Inc., 2 West 46th Street, New York, New York, and Visual Art Industries, 68–33rd Street, Brooklyn, New York. A limited selection also is usually available in hardware and paint stores.

Stencil lettering sets consist of a cardboard or metal stencil card containing the alphabet and other characters. Stencil guides may be purchased in various type faces and sizes. The cardboard guides are inexpensive, but neat results are difficult. Metal guides are more durable but present the same problems of positioning and even impression. Stencil sets are available from school supply houses and office supply firms. The stencil sign maker is a sophisticated metal stencil. Each letter is separate. Words are made by arranging the letters in a special metal holder. This system is quick and inexpensive, but the initial cost is fairly high. The sign maker is available from school supply houses and office supply firms.

Sticky letters are thin paper letters with an adhesive backing that sticks when moistened. They are not re-usable, and they come in complete sets of several sizes and colors. These letters are rather expensive but have a very professional appearance and are particularly suited for signs. One source is Stik-a-Letter Company, Route 2, Box 1400, Escondido, California.

Tape letters are produced on a hand-operated machine. The letters produced are small and appear on a plastic tape that has an adhesive backing. They are particularly useful in labeling individual items in a display. The initial cost for a heavy duty machine is rather high, but operating costs are similar to those of light, inexpensive models. The latter uses a narrow tape and tends to break down under hard use. Department and hardware stores carry several brands of label-making machines.

Wood letters are available in the basic alphabet with the most used letters being repeated several times. Wood letters are useful for novelty displays and may be helpful in teaching upper-case letters by the kinesthetic method. These letters, which are rather expensive, are available from school supply firms.

Free and Inexpensive Materials. All teachers are interested in materials that are readily available and free of charge. These materials offer many opportunities for instructional reinforcement as they tend to be quite colorful and decorative. Many free materials do have disadvantages that should be considered before they are ordered or used. Slow learners usually find free materials unsuitable for independent reading. The materials lack controlled vocabularies, do not limit the number of new ideas introduced, and are written at high reading levels. The teacher may overcome these problems by reading the materials aloud and asking students to reproduce the content through their own blackboard or notebook stories. The teacher may also use the free materials to prepare reading selections for duplication. Free materials often have a commercial story to tell that may not expose students to the entire truth. The teacher may find two materials that tell different stories and use them for comparison. He may also begin a presentation with an unbiased, balanced picture of a topic and then introduce the commercial material to contrast a narrow or divergent point of view. Another problem with free materials is that they rarely fit neatly into an established curriculum plan, and their introduction often appears artificial. Use of the unit plan may help here, particularly if the materials relate to topics that hold special interest for students.

Despite the problems inherent in their use, free and inexpensive materials are a welcomed addition to a program planned for slow learners. The following list includes some of the most popular publications listing free and inexpensive materials for classroom use. These references are available at most college and school curriculum libraries, or they may be purchased. When ordering materials, be sure to include information such as class size and class level. The best way to ensure a response to your request is to write a personal letter on school stationery.

Guides to Free and Inexpensive Materials

1. Elementary Teachers Guide to Free and Inexpensive Curriculum Materials, Educators Progress Service, Randolph, Wisconsin, published yearly. The Educators Progress Service also publishes guides to free materials in science, social studies, and other subject areas.
2. Sources of Free and Inexpensive Educational Materials, Second Edition, 1962, revised, 1963, compiled and edited by Esther Dever, P.O. Box 186, Grafton, West Virginia.

3. Educators Progress Service, Randolph, Wisconsin
   Educators Guide to Free Filmstrips
   Educators Guide to Free Films
   Educators Guide to Free Tapes, Scripts, Transcriptions
   Published yearly.
4. *The Instructor*
5. *The Grade Teacher*
6. *Exceptional Children*
7. *Industrial Arts and Vocational Education*

The last four guides are periodicals that carry listings of free and inexpensive materials; these periodicals are available in most libraries.

Teacher-made Reading Materials. The quantity and quality of reading materials for slow learners grows steadily. However, the teacher is frequently required to write his own material for use in a unit or for reading practice. The following suggestions for the development of teacher-made reading materials are adapted from Featherstone [126]:

1. Select a topic that is related to a unit, a matter of class interest or a subject within the experience of the group.
2. Determine what purpose you want your selection to serve. Will it present new vocabulary, teach a new concept, review past experiences, or serve other goals?
3. Write a rough draft: keep a natural style; consider the children's language and experience; keep new words somewhat limited (approximately 5–10 to a page, depending on level); introduce words above reading level only if they are important, motivating and taught separately; write approximately one level below the one you wish eventually to reach.
4. Check the vocabulary with a standard reference: Basal reader word lists, Thorndike word list,* Gates word list.†
5. Submit the completed draft to one or more children of known reading level. Have them read aloud without assistance. Note interest shown. Note difficult words or sentences. Note any comments of the reader that might indicate necessary revisions.
6. Rewrite material as necessary and prepare a revised draft for class use.

* Edward L. Thorndike and Irving Lorge, *The Teachers Word Book of 30,000 Words* (New York: Teachers College Press, 1944).

† Arthur I. Gates, *A Reading Vocabulary for the Primary Grades* (New York Teachers College Press, 1935).

CHAPTER VII

Educational Innovation and Slow Learning

Educational innovation is a rather endless topic in this time of great ferment in the American school. New developments in instruction seem to be reported daily; the teacher hardly has time to master one new technique before something newer is introduced. The widely held opinion that it takes fifty years to fully incorporate social innovations into the school program appears to have been altered considerably by the pace at which schools now adopt the hardware and software of the new technology. On the surface, at least, the American school represents one of the world's most modern, most technology conscious, and most rapidly changing educational systems.

In addition to computerizing its role in society, the American school appears to be broadening it. The move to increased diversity of purpose is evident in the introduction of preschool classes for deprived youth, the growing number of after-school remedial programs, the special summer programs for the educationally disadvantaged, the burgeoning school work-study classes, the membership of teachers in unions, the increasing involvement of neighborhood groups in school planning, and the appointment of full- and part-time school personnel to establish and maintain liaison with community groups and agencies.

All of the new programs, of course, are not entirely welcome by everyone connected with education; nor are all of the ideas in current circulation entirely novel or entirely sound. In most cases, the tune is familiar; it is only the words that are new. It is extremely difficult for the teacher to decide upon the ideas he can accept and those he must resist, what techniques he should try at once and which he should set aside for later consideration. The task becomes even more complicated when the slow learner is considered. Many newer teaching techniques have only been evaluated grossly with the general school population. There has been little time to conduct definitive research with such specialized groups as slow learners.

To help the teacher select and apply educational innovations in slow learning, this chapter reviews several topics to which educators have given considerable recent attention. The selection is made with conscious realization that some of the topics mentioned may fade from attention very rapidly while those not included may gain prominence and permanence. Such is the business of soothsaying.

NONGRADED CLASSES

According to a statement in the December, 1965, issue of *Phi Delta Kappan,* one of every three large American school systems was, at that time, using a nongraded sequence in at least some of its elementary schools. The adoption of nongrading would appear to be increasing as a search is made for ways to implement the long-neglected concept of individual differences. The nongraded system is advocated because it supposedly eliminates the need for all children to learn the same material at approximately the same time. Nongrading substitutes a flexible grouping plan for the rather rigid confines of the traditional grades.

The most common form of elementary school nongrading is the three-year sequence. The child's progress is measured by his achievement in reading. As he accomplishes a specified amount of work, he is moved to a higher level where material of increasing difficulty is presented. The pupil's movement from group to group is without specific time limits or formal promotion procedure. The rapid learner may complete the three-year sequence in two years, while it may take the slow learner four years to achieve the same result [Hillson, 44]. Nongrading requires some administrative adjustments, particularly in communicating the change to parents, reporting pupil progress, providing a wider variety of learning materials to each class, and training teachers to think about students without having to refer to grade labels.

Nongrading originated in the primary level, and when it is adopted by a system tends to be instituted first at that level. An increasing number of schools are experimenting with nongrading in the intermediate school years, and a few systems report nongrading experiments at the junior and senior high school.

Nongrading at first glance appears to offer slow learners several distinct advantages over the traditional school organization—it removes the failure and frustration associated with "staying back"; it tends to produce small homogeneous groups within larger groups thus gaining the advantages of homogeneity while avoiding the stigma; and it reduces pressure for specific achievement while allowing the student the general intellectual stimulation provided by the presence of normal and bright peers. Since nongrading implies small group rather than mass group teaching, there is greater possibility that the slow learner will receive more individual attention.

The advantages of nongrading for slow learners may lead teachers to promote its adoption in their own school systems. While this interest in nongrading should not be discouraged. it should be tempered by the knowledge that nongrading, like all things devised by man, is not perfect. Nongrading may simply be a means of replacing familiar problems with a more exotic species. Nongrading allows the teacher to pay more attention to slow learners, but this system points up very clearly that most of the instructional materials presently available are not suitable for use in a program that stresses attention to individual differences and uses a flexible grouping plan. To fill the gap, the teacher may drill with familiar materials or provide unrelated materials for enrichment. Whatever alternative is selected, the absence of enough appropriate materials tends to negate the advantages of nongrading. The problem will not be solved until teachers have enough time and training to produce their own materials.

Nongrading changes the traditional organization of the school. It also changes the demands made upon the teacher and requires the school system to alter its basic educational philosophy. Teachers who, for many years, have performed in a certain way tend to continue this pattern after specific grade designation is removed from their titles, thus negating the inherent advantages of nongrading. For example, when students repeat levels instead of grades, one rigid standard is replaced by another. The school system may also destroy the positive advantages of nongrading by adopting the system for the wrong reasons. As an example, the school system that decides on nongrading because it feels such a plan will allow brighter students to cover more subject content may possibly overbalance the program to the detriment of slower students.

It would appear that nongrading holds promise for slow learners if its adoption reflects the goal of providing the best possible education for all learners at their own rate of intellecual growth.

PROGRAMMED INSTRUCTION

Programmed instruction is a method for individualizing learning by making it systematic and by matching instructional plans to what is known about how people learn. Programming provides material with which the student can interact and learn from without requiring the direct assistance of other learners or the instructor. Depending on its design, a program may move a student forward in minute steps that preclude failure, or it may permit him to take intuitive leaps as he desires. Either type of programming depends upon the immediate display of information for reward and reinforcement. Programming is sometimes accomplished with complex apparatus, thus the popular conception of teaching machines. With increasing frequency, however, programs are being produced in textbook or workbook format, and the teacher of slow learners is more likely to use a programmed text than to use a teaching machine. Programming offers slow learners the opportunity to learn at their own pace without the constant intervention of an adult whose presence may threaten the student. Because the student's responses are not given in a group setting, he need not fear that others will immediately be aware of his failure. Also, the use of individual programs permits each child to study only that material in which he is deficient and thus avoids material that is too easy or too difficult.

The programmed learning experiments conducted with slow learners thus far indicate that slow students tend to accomplish more when their programs are presented in very small steps and the margin for failure has been reduced to the minimum. This approach, called linear programming, seems to provide slow learners with the security they have not found in other types of instruction. It also appears to allow the time and structure necessary for building insights. Branching programs that allow for student choice make failure responses possible. Consequently, branching programs may be rejected because they remind the slow learner of past situations where his efforts have produced only failure. Programmed instruction demands intense individual attention and places great emphasis on a person's self-dependence. Slow learners tend to devaluate themselves, to be personally insecure, and to be distrustful of their own responses to instructional stimuli. It is not surprising that slow learners are reported to cheat more on programmed texts than is normal and to request teacher support despite the program's ability to remove the teacher from the learning situation [Reid, 71].

Available research indicates that programmed learning is a useful tool for teaching slow learners and may produce higher achievement levels than do conventional methods. The positive benefits of programming are not generally available to slow learners, however, because the concept is not self-implementing. The programmed materials in common use present problems identical to those that plague the slow learner whenever he opens a text. The reading level of the programs is often beyond his comprehension, the idea content may be outside his experience, and the material frequently moves too quickly.

If the slow child is to profit from programming, he must have programs that he can understand and that lead him gradually from one item of knowledge to the next. The development of such programs is not an easy task. It requires the combined talents of an experienced programmer and an experienced teacher and a market that will make the effort profitable. The teacher of slow learners may find it useful to investigate the programmed material that has been developed for teaching levels below his own and to refer to the growing literature on the use of programmed materials with the culturally deprived and the mentally retarded. The teacher may also attempt to develop competency in writing programs although this alternative is quite beyond the resources or backgrounds of many teachers.

Unlike some other educational innovations whose eventual impact is in doubt, programmed learning appears to have a permanent place in the schools. If exploited fully, it may eventually revolutionalize their operation and function and, as a by-product, reduce substantially the problem of slow learning.

READING INNOVATIONS: I.T.A.

One of the approaches to reading instruction that has stimulated much experiment and argument is the initial teaching alphabet. This recently popularized method of reading instruction was originally developed by Pitman in England. A special alphabet of forty-four symbols is used to simplify the task of teaching beginning reading and spelling to young children. Small and large versions of the same symbol (s, S) are employed so that no uppercase alphabet must be learned. The initial teaching alphabet is said to make it possible to reduce from 2,000 to 88 the number of visual patterns the child must use in reproducing the approximately forty sounds of English speech. Consequently, the child has fewer opportunities for failure, and, theoretically, he can acquire a basic reading vocabulary more rapidly and with less frustration than through conventional teaching methods. The i.t.a. method requires eventual transfer to traditional symbols and reading procedures, but its proponents claim that transfer is easier than teaching the traditional system in the first place.

As a basic approach to reading, the initial teaching alphabet would appear to be an attractive method for slow learners. Seemingly, it can help reduce early failure and provide a structure to which slow learners respond more readily. In addition, the novelty and sequential features of i.t.a. might be expected to make it an important tool for use in remedial instruction with older students.

Downing [25] reports that the initial English experiments with i.t.a. indicate that there are fewer poor performers in beginning reading in i.t.a. classes than in traditional classes. He notes also that there are some slow children who will not be able to read at the expected age even with the simple, systematic i.t.a. process. Although the promise of i.t.a. has been recognized by many teachers of the mentally retarded and slow learners, their classroom efforts have not generally been conducted in a manner that makes their results suitable for careful evaluation. Several studies of i.t.a. on general populations have considered its effects on the slow learner, but the resulting reports are too conflicting to allow generalization. In a summary of i.t.a. research, Gilhooly [35] concludes that i.t.a. is no more effective in teaching reading to dull children than are traditional methods. In dissent, however, Mazurkiewicz [Dolmatch and Mazurkiewicz, 24] indicates that when the slowest students (I.Q. 50–75) in his project group transferred to the traditional alphabet after approximately two years of i.t.a. instruction, they were reading second-grade material, a feat he considers remarkable.

The teacher who considers using i.t.a. for his slower students should first become familiar with its purposes and procedures. He should plan his application of the method so that he will be able to measure results. The same immaturity that handicaps the slow child in traditional reading methods may also affect his responses to i.t.a. The slow student's difficulty in making abstractions may impair his ability to learn the i.t.a. symbols and to make the necessary transition between these symbols and the traditional alphabet. The older student may learn to read through the use of i.t.a. because his increased maturity and approaching employment provide the necessary motivation and ability. These factors may also result in his learning through conventional methods that are carefully presented.

The i.t.a. is still an experimental approach for the slow learner and must be used in the manner of all experiments. It is too early to accept or reject i.t.a. on the basis of the decibel level of the argument surrounding its use. In no event should the teacher use i.t.a. unless he has a thorough grounding in the teaching of conventional reading and spelling.

SCHOOL WORK-STUDY PROGRAMS

The school work-study program is a systematic approach to bridging the gap between the world of the school with its specific tasks and the world of work where the prescribed tasks are quite different. Within the space of two or three years, the school work-study program moves the student from full-time classroom work with minor vocational content to a half-day school, half-day work program that has heavy vocational emphasis. Students are generally paid for their part-time work, and its completion is considered to fulfill part of the graduation requirement.

School work-study programs have existed in the United States for approximately sixty years. During that time various kinds of programs have been developed to meet the needs of different types of learners. It is expected that since the inception of school work-study programs, a fair number of slow learners have become work-study graduates, although programs designed specifically for slow students are a fairly recent development.

The slow learner in secondary school often is simply waiting to terminate his school career as soon as the law allows. He is uncertain or perhaps unconcerned about his post-school future. He is preoccupied with the feeling that school is an unpleasant place, that it fails to satisfy many of his wishes, and that it makes him feel rejected. The schools recognize this feeling and have placed great emphasis on preventing dropouts. Unfortunately, however, most of these preventive measures mean little unless the school provides a program that the student considers a worthwhile alternative to dropping out. One of the programs that has been proposed as an attractive alternate to dropping out is the school work-study program. It does have limitations, however, and is not the answer for all slow learners—it should not be thought of as instant panacea. The school work-study program should be one of several secondary school programming alternatives available to slow learners. They should be able to enroll in remedial academic programs that lead to post high school technical training, appropriate trade training courses, special vocational schools, and the like. The school work-study program should be thought of as an alternative to various school programs, not the only alternate to the college preparatory curriculum.

The school system that considers establishing a school work-study program should be certain that the program's vocational base is broad enough so that slow learners are not trained only for jobs that match their stereotypes. Program plans must also be founded on the realization that the teacher will not have the time nor training to make vocational placements for all students. He should have the assistance of a counselor or coordinator whose primary task is placement and who is also responsible for providing the field feedback so necessary to effective class instruction. The program should have definite admission standards that ensure a reasonable percentage of student employment. It is also necessary to allow credit flexibility. Students should be able to leave school when they are ready for work even though graduation time has not come. If necessary, they should also be able to remain in school without stigma after graduation time has passed.

One of the most consistent statements applicable to the topic of educational innovation is that reliable research results are few. Happily, this statement is not entirely true when used in the discussion of school work-study programs. No great volume of research does exist, but several projects just completed or in progress are the source of rather definitive information.

Karnes [51] reports on a school work-study project in which ninety-one matched pairs of subjects, age thirteen to nineteen, were used to test the effectiveness of a special prevocational curriculum in reducing dropouts, improving attendance, reducing involvements with legal authorities, and increasing employment potential. The program emphasizes the provision of complete diagnostic, treatment, and counseling services so that each student's educational plan may be tailored to his exact needs. Particular stress is placed on utilizing the counselor from the state division of vocational rehabilitation. He provides vocational and personal counseling to slow students before they leave school and is actively involved in school decisions related to future vocational planning. The program uses an in-school workroom to provide closely supervised work situations in conjunction with an in-school work counselor. The provision of social casework services to the experimental group is another feature of the program. A program for training customer check-out clerks constitutes one of the experiment's specific work training stations. Most preparatory activities are general in nature and do not train for specific occupations. The results of the program indicate that the student's possibility of achieving successful employment is directly related to his age and length of time in the program. The most unstable group of part-time employees consists of sixteen- and seventeen-year-old students. Early results indicate that the program not only reduces dropouts, but it increases the student's desire to obtain further education. The movement of students from the high school program to a vocational school for trade training is apparently much more frequent than is customary for slow learners.

A more current report of a school work-study program is provided by Becken [9]. This project, conducted in Medford, Oregon, is designed to improve academic achievement through use of a team teaching plan, to make a specific determination of community job opportunities for slow learners, and to prepare students for the jobs that are found. Other features include the extensive use of counseling personnel, the establishment of a job placement service, and the provision of an adult education program for previous dropouts.

The Medford program is very definite in taking a positive approach to curriculum development and stresses that the program is preparatory rather than preventive. It is not based on any dire predictions of drastic consequences but is founded on the conviction that slow learners can achieve good vocational adjustment if they are given a sound program of vocational preparation. The plan for achieving the program's objectives is very highly developed and finely detailed. It includes considerable attention to the utilization of community resources and emphasizes the fact that the program cannot begin and end in the school. The plan also stresses the need for developing ideas that can be disseminated and cross-checked easily in many communities across the country. The program has recently completed its preliminary process of information gathering and initial planning, and it is moving into its operational stage.

Quincy, Illinois, has also initiated a special program for slow learners. Its uniqueness lies in the fact that it is planned for grades 7 through 12 [Matthews and Sorenson, 62]. The preventive theme is strong in this program since the research was given impetus by an earlier study showing that school dropouts tend to evidence poor intellectual performance, have a long history of school failure, and are unable to find part-time employment that might relieve some of the pressures they experience in school. Positive attitude development is a prime objective of the Quincy program as is the formulation of a curriculum that promotes vocational preparedness. An effort is also made to involve the parents and thus reduce any negative effect that they may have on the student's school performance. Special features of this project are its mention of the need to facilitate the slow learner's transition between various levels of the school, the need to define the role of the teacher and to improve his effectiveness in achieving it, and the statement of specific objectives that are to be used in program evaluation. A block system of grouping is used to provide students with as much regular classwork as is commensurate with their over-all maturity. Emphasis is placed on activities drawn from the environment, and instruction is related to the exploration of vocational possibilities. A number of part-time work-study experiences are included. These experiences utilize settings in school, in business, and in a school-operated training center (service station).

The Quincy experiment appears to be very complete in its design; it seems to consider very specifically the needs of a well-described local population.

The three research and demonstration projects described are supported in whole, or in part, by federal grants. There are, of course, many other programs not supported by grant funds that are experiencing a great deal of success with the school work-study approach. Teachers interested in school work-study should seek information on local programs from their state education department.

INNOVATIONS FROM SPECIAL EDUCATION

The field of special education has, for many years, produced instructional innovations that have found their way into general education with very little fanfare or acknowledgment of their source. It would appear that there are several recent developments in various areas of special education that may follow this pattern. Those innovations that seem to have possible applications to slow learners in the near future are treated briefly here.

Auditory Input Training. The term "auditory input training" refers to the use of a magnetic tape or other source of recorded sound to present specific information in an individual setting. Experiments with this type of teaching are being conducted in several areas of special education. Most of these experiments are informal. They seem to develop almost spontaneously as the teacher becomes aware of the fact that a child will attend to a verbal message much more intently when it is presented through earphones than when the same information is presented by the teacher in a group setting. Most teachers who experiment with auditory input training use an earphone-equipped tape recorder. The student listens at a desk that has been placed behind a sound-absorbing screen. The setting suggests a language laboratory, and some teachers have actually used their school's language instruction facilities for auditory input training.

Auditory input training has been applied in several ways. Some teachers record stories from a text used in class and then ask students to read the same story while listening to it on tape. On the same tape, students also are asked comprehension questions. Some teachers use the technique in conjunction with workbooks. The taped message tells the student on what page to begin, repeats the necessary directions several times, and may, after a suitable pause, provide the correct answers. One teacher assigns retarded students to the tape recorder corner for an hour at a time. During this period, the prerecorded tape presents arithmetic problems or assignments in workbooks. While the student completes the given problems or assignments, the tape plays popular music. Teachers of disturbed or hyperactive children find that the taped lessons have a calming effect as they allow the student to reduce the personal contacts that threaten or distract him. The auditory input technique is also used to describe filmstrips that are captioned at a high reading level or carry no captions at all.

The slow learner would appear to profit from the auditory input techniques used with retarded or disturbed students. Usually the required equipment is not difficult to obtain, and most classrooms have some suitable space where the addition of a simple screen to reduce distraction is the only requirement. At present, there are few, if any, commercially available materials for use in auditory input training. The teacher must make all his tapes, which is a time-consuming task. Also, most teachers do not ordinarily teach in the systematic manner demanded by an effective tape. The creative teacher of slow learners may find ways of making suitable tapes by recording class discussions and adding questions to be answered, by having good readers make tapes, or by pooling taped lessons with other teachers. Auditory input is a potentially valuable technique for teaching slow students and should be further explored.

Compressed and Expanded Speech. Considerable research has been devoted to the electromechanical alteration of the presentation rate of recorded verbal communication. This technique is described as compressed speech when the presentation speed is increased and as expanded speech when the presentation speed is decreased. Both alterations are accomplished by subjecting ordinary taped speech to a special process that uses electronic and mechanical means to lengthen or shorten certain speech sounds. The resulting recording retains the original pitch and tone quality, but the rate of presentation is more rapid or slow. The process requires special equipment, but the resulting tapes or records can be played on standard machines.

Both compressed and expanded speech have been applied to the education of exceptional children. Compressed speech has been applied most often in the field of visual impairment. Persons unable to read print books have two avenues of communication available—they can listen and learn, or they can learn tactically by reading Braille. Both methods are much less efficient than reading from print and tend to make it impossible for the visually impaired to learn quickly, even when their intelligence levels are similar to those of the nonhandicapped. Compressed speech allows considerably more information to be presented in a specified time period. Accordingly, it can help the visually impaired increase their learning rate. Since compressed speech is variable in its rate of presentation, the visually impaired person can gradually build his listening speed. He may also select presentation speeds according to the type of material being used. Experiments with the blind indicate that the rate of presentation may be increased to 300 words per minute (double the noncompressed rate) with no comprehension problems. Rates as high as 475 words per minute have been used with subjects who have had considerable practice [Orr and Friedman, 67].

Many slow learners are quite familiar with and proficient in the language of poverty and slum living. This language, with its extreme economy of words and its frequent use of expressive sounds, is, in itself, a variant of compressed speech. From this corollary it might be assumed that slow learners are capable of developing an understanding of compressed speech. There is no information, however, to indicate how interested they would be in attempting such learning. If slow learners could be motivated to learn the use of compressed speech, several positive results are possible. It might be found that compressed speech provides practice in careful listening and sequential thinking; also, by bypassing weak reading skills, it may allow students more time to develop the confidence and verbal facility so necessary to effective reading. Compressed speech may be used to present review materials, or it may simply have enough novelty value to provide the motivation necessary to learning. Compressed speech can also be presented simultaneously with reading materials. At first the oral presentation will be keyed to the student's reading rate. It will be speeded up gradually to stimulate him to read faster. Undoubtedly, compressed speech is an innovation that requires a careful trial with slow learners.

Expanded speech has been proposed as a possible aid in educating the mentally retarded. It has been used experimentally in some special classes, but no well-documented studies of its use are available. Expanded speech might be useful in helping slow learners develop listening skills by hearing how pronunciation is formed. It might also lessen the pressure to hear every word that is spoken and thus give them more time for comprehension. It could be used to retard the sound tracks of motion pictures, most of which move too rapidly for the slower child.

The electromechanical alteration of presented speech rate is an innovation that has found promising uses in special education. It certainly should be the subject of experimentation in the field of slow learning. Persons wishing to hear examples of compressed speech are referred to the several companies that produce the necessary equipment. One company offering a free sample recording is Infotronic Systems, Inc., 2 West 46th Street, New York, New York, 10036.

Perceptual Development Materials. Special educators have, in recent years, produced a variety of materials designed to help young children improve perceptual skills. These materials have been generated in particular by the growing concern for brain-damaged children and children described as having general learning difficulties. Experiments with preschool mentally retarded children have also resulted in the development of perceptual training programs. The attention given to early perception training as a method of overcoming learning problems has a long history that includes such names as Itard, Sequin, and Montessori. During this history, various techniques have been developed, have had brief periods of intense popularity, and have then all but disappeared from general use. Recently, the interest in perceptual training has had a renaissance. This probably results primarily from the fact that modern materials are relatively inexpensive, quickly produced, and easily used. For example, the Frostig program for training visual perception is sold in the form of spirit duplicator masters. These can be readily run off as needed [Frostig and Horne, 33]. The material developed by Goldstein and Levitt [38] is sold in sets that provide individual practice in developing a specific skill. The teacher's interest in the modern materials is also related to the fact that most are accompanied by step-by-step instructions and information useful in making an educational diagnosis.

There is strong reason to believe that young children suspected of being slow should be exposed to a thorough program of perceptual training. This exposure will allow the teacher to gain a complete idea of the student's learning problems, and it will replace the familiar shotgun pattern of many readiness programs with a clear systematic attack on the child's difficulties.

TEAM TEACHING

Team teaching, like slow learning, suffers from the lack of a precise definition. Since teams are organized for different philosophical and administrative reasons, the resulting structures are difficult to compare in definite terms. Accordingly, it is impossible to evaluate the total effect of the many current team teaching experiments.

The proponents of team teaching appear to agree that it is designed to improve education by utilizing the teacher's time more efficiently. Team teaching also attempts to make the most effective use of an individual teacher's special talents or competencies and provides a structure in which students may be grouped flexibly.

As generally used, the term "team teaching" implies that two or more instructional personnel will work cooperatively to teach groups of various sizes. The team generally includes teaching and clerical personnel. The teaching positions are often arranged in hierarchical order according to expected competencies and responsibilities but several other arrangements also are possible [Drummond, 27]. The teaching hierarchy may consist of a team leader, master teachers, assistant teachers, and teachers' helpers. All hierarchical teams are not so well-organized, and the types of personnel used will depend on a team's size and complexity. Another arrangement is the cooperative team where all teachers have equal rank and work together to solve mutual problems. Whatever organizational pattern is used, the team concept requires constant interaction between team members.

Team teaching is an approach to more effective instruction for all children, and if special groups, such as slow learners, are considered, they are included within the total discussion. An analysis of this discussion indicates that team teaching may be helpful to slow learners because it allows some teachers to provide remedial instruction to small groups of pupils while other teachers instruct large groups. The fact that several teachers have an opportunity to observe students in various situations and to discuss their observations in depth may make it more possible to plan an over-all program for the slow student that is sequential and well-coordinated. The regrouping process inherent in the team ensures that slow students will meet superior teachers and will not be assigned completely to an instructor who is not considered competent enough to teach regular learners. Regrouping also allows the slow student to come into contact with more rapid learners in situations that do not create harmful competition.

On the negative side, team teaching may easily produce subject matter specialists who are unable or unwilling to provide slow learners with the general academic skills that they require. This problem is particularly acute in the secondary school. Not all team instruction can be given in small groups, and there is the possibility that slow learners may become lost in large-group sessions. In the early school years, the slow learner may not be mature enough to adapt to the number of different teachers who face him each day. The teachers may come to know the slow learner, but the slow learner may never have an opportunity to know the teachers. Also, the concept of team teaching requires curriculum revision as well as organizational revision, and such revision has been notoriously nonexistent regardless of the administrative context in which slow learners are considered.

Team teaching is not a concept developed specifically for slow learners but an innovation in which their involvement may result in some advantages. Those persons interested in slow learning should investigate existing or proposed team organizations to ensure that the slow child's needs will be considered. Team teaching can be a fruitful tool for slow learners if it is not allowed to follow the example of other innovations and pay but lip service to his needs.

APPENDIX A

Suggested Teaching Materials for Use with Slow Learners

An annotated list arranged by subject matter areas

Most publishers of books and other instructional aids must, of economic necessity, prepare their materials for the largest possible audience and consider qualities that will increase saleability. Consequently, the relatively few materials designed specifically to meet the problem of slow learning tend to be oriented to the broadest possible interpretation of the general definition. These materials also appear to stress the idea that their use will improve, increase, or otherwise positively affect the student's ability to learn. Understandably, when these materials are used in a program that adheres to the concept of diagnostic teaching, their use tends to be rather limited and their results are generally considered to be only superficially effective. A few publishers have devoted themselves to producing materials only for slow learners, thus building the specialized identification that is useful to a limited market. These publishers, however, usually lack the means to conduct field testing and to exercise production controls that are required for the development of high-quality materials. Because of the present economic facts of materials publishing, there are some very general and not-too-useful materials of high quality and a few materials of specific interest that are of poor quality. While admitting that the present crop of materials that can be used with slow learners is not what it might be, it is important to note that some instructional help is better than none and that, as publishers recognize and develop their market in slow learning, the materials picture is certain to brighten considerably.

MATERIALS SELECTION

The teacher has three general sources from which to select materials for slow learners. The most abundant source is the store of materials developed for use with the mentally retarded. Materials developed specifically for slow learners comprise the second largest source. A third source is the collection of materials prepared for normal students, some of which has inherent features that meet the slow child's needs.

Since present conditions make it impossible to generalize recommendations on any material, the teacher is cautioned to look at each of the items listed below with extreme care. Some will be suitable; many, even when labeled "for slow learners," will not. The following criteria are suggested for evaluating these and other materials before adopting them for class use.

1. The material should have a unique appeal to the slow learner. This uniqueness may be related to speed of presentation, concreteness, novelty of approach, or similar aspects that are clearly designed to meet the slow child's accepted learning characteristics. Novelty alone does not satisfy this criterion.
2. Proved instructional practices should be adhered to. Materials for slow learners cannot violate standard educational practices on the premise that such learners are "special." If unorthodox procedures or methods are included in the materials under review, suitable evidence must be presented that supports scientifically their use and effectivenesss with slow learners.
3. The materials should respect the self-concept of the student for whom they are recommended. This respect should be reflected in the material's language, subject matter, and in any related activities that are suggested. The teacher must weigh the student's actual social age against his known academic achievement in applying this criteria and be certain to look beyond the labels.
4. The materials should be well written. This criteria implies good literary quality.
5. Production standards should be equal to those found in the standard school text. Poorly printed and bound books further limit the student's learning environment and may also increase his feelings of being rejected.
6. The materials should be comparable in price to regular materials. Exception should be made only if the materials have obvious features that justify a higher price. Such features might include unusually complete illustrations, supplementary film strips, unusual but necessary packaging, or the like.

7. The material must be broad enough in its concept to provide for individual differences within a classroom. Too often, "special" materials become overly special and exclude all but a small number of students.
8. The materials should reflect careful development and testing. This should be documented in the teacher's guide.

Bibliographic categories included in the following listing are:

1. English and literature
2. Language development
3. Mathematics
4. Reading
5. Science
6. Social studies
7. Social and vocational development
8. Teacher resources

Bibliographical abbreviations used in the listing include:

1. "Paper W.B." indicates a workbook format in paper binding. Items not noted as paper may be assumed to be hard cover.
2. **I.L.** indicates approximate interest level.
3. **R.L.** indicates reading level. When a specific formula has been used, this is indicated.
4. **A.L.** indicates achievement level.

Adapted Classics, New York: Globe Book Company.

I.L.: junior and senior high school **R.L.:** varies from grades 5–8

Approximately fifty titles from classical literature. All have been adapted in terms of lowering vocabulary level and removing very abstract passages. Some available in paperback.

Carlin, Christ, and Holder. *English on the Job,* Book 1; Carlin and Holder, Book 2; New York: Globe Book Company.

I.L.: senior high school

A course of basic English for the non-college-bound. Attempts to relate academics to the student's interest in employment. Includes tests and drills. Emphasis is on functional grammar and vocational guidance.

Gershenfeld and Burton. *Stories for Teen-agers,* Book A; Burton and Mersand, Books I and 2; New York: Globe Book Company.

I.L.: junior and senior high school **R.L.:** Book A: grade 4
Books 1 and 2: grades 5–6

Collection of stories written for teen interests by modern writers. All chosen from current periodicals. Includes aids for improving reading skills.

Individualized English, Chicago, Illinois: Follett Publishing Company.

Set J: junior high school **Set H:** senior high school

Programmed exercise cards, answer sheets, and mastery tests. Advertised as general material that is flexible enough to be used at all ability levels. Not designed specifically for the slow learner. No specific information available on its effectiveness with this group.

Jochen and Shapiro. *Vocational English,* Books 1 and 2, New York: Globe Book Company.

I.L.: senior high school

A series designed to teach language skills to the non-college bound student. Pretest and achievement tests for each unit are included with this series.

Learning Your Language/One, Chicago, Illinois: Follett Publishing Company. (Paper W.B.)

I.L.: junior high school **R.L.:** grades 3–5–6–9

Six booklets designed to improve reading comprehension as basic language skills are developed. Uses stories and test situations. Specifically designed for slow learners.

Marcatante and Potter. *American Folklore and Legends,* New York: Globe Book Company.

I.L.: senior high school **R.L.:** grade 4

Adapted stories from American heritage. Student exercises included; teacher manual available.

Potter and Robinson. *Myths and Folk Tales Around the World,* New York: Globe Book Company.

I.L.: senior high school **R.L.:** grade 4

Adapted stories from classical literature. Includes exercises; teacher manual available.

Schleyen. *Stories for Today's Youth,* Book 1, New York: Globe Book Company.

I.L.: junior and senior high school **R.L.:** grades 4–5

A collection of stories written about city adolescents in an integrated setting. Reading aids are included.

Woolf and Wellemeyer. *Journeys in Reading,* Books 1 and 2, New York: Globe Book Company.

I.L.: junior high school **R.L.:** grades 5–7

Anthologies of well-known plays, poems, short stories, and other literary selections chosen for their low reading level. No adaptations or abridgments. Color illustrations; teacher manual available.

LANGUAGE DEVELOPMENT

Functional Core Vocabulary for Slow Learners, Robert Burger, P.O. Box 165, Rensselaer, New York.

2,585 words reflecting experience levels rather than grade levels. Guide for vocabulary in preparing reading materials. Words from standard word lists plus essential words involved in studying New York City cores plus some vocational words. Although some of the words are peculiar to New York City, teachers in other areas may find it possible to adapt.

The Noisy Books, New York: Harper & Row Publishers.

These books are quite useful for stimulating language. This publisher has a number of other "read aloud" books.

Read Aloud Books, Chicago, Illinois: Follett Publishing Company.

I.L.: kindergarten–grades 3 or 4 **R.L.:** upper half of grade 3

A selection of forty-one books chosen for their interest and ability to be read easily to children who need to develop listening skills and to have their listening vocabularies enriched. Includes the more familiar children's classics as well as a number of contemporary titles. Originally drawn up as a list for use in project head start programs.

Russell and Russell. *Listening Aids through the Grades,* New York: Teachers College Press.

A book of 190 listening activities that may be used by the teacher to build language skills at all grade levels.

Slepian and Seidler. *Listen-Hear Books,* Chicago, Illinois: Follett Publishing Company.

I.L.: kindergarten–grade 2 **R.L.:** grade 3

A series of six books. Each book is designed to teach correct sounding of one of five consonants and one dipthong that cause problems for some children. Not designed specifically for slow learners but may be useful in overcoming minor pronunciation problems. Designed to be read aloud.

Success in Language/A, Chicago, Illinois: Follett Publishing Company. (Paper W.B.)

I.L.: junior and senior high school

A set of eight booklets. Advertised as having been developed for slow learners. Designed to improve communication in all areas.

MATHEMATICS

Basic Modern Mathematics, Palo Alto, California: Addison-Wesley School Division.

I.L.: junior high school **R.L.:** approximately grade 5

A book designed specifically for the slow learner. An attempt has been made to increase the learner's success by reducing the reading level and by including many illustrations.

Every Day Business, Gary D. Lawson, 9488 Sara Street, Elk Grove, California. (Paper W.B.)

I.L.: senior high school **R.L.:** grade 4

Includes work on banking, buying, income tax, insurance, budgeting. An overview of common adult activities. Developed for the mentally retarded.

Figure It Out, Books 1 and 2, Chicago, Illinois: Follett Publishing Company. (Paper W.B.)

I.L.: adult or young adult **R.L.:** Book 1: grades 0–4
Book 2: grades 5–8

An expanding series of books containing graded problems in traditional arithmetic.

Getting Ready for Pay Day, Frank E. Richards, 215 Church Street, Phoenix, New York.

I.L.: senior high school **R.L.:** upper half of grade 4

Part 1: Checking Accounts
Part II: Savings Accounts
Part III: Planning Ahead

Mathematics in Living, Pruett Press, Inc., Boulder, Colorado.

I.L.: senior high school

Book I: Buying
Book II: Wages and Budgets
Book III: Banking and Loans
Book IV: Insurance and Taxes

Money Makes Sense, Fearon Publishers, 828 Valencia Street, San Francisco, California. (Paper W.B.)

I.L.: junior and senior high school **A.L.:** grades 1–3

A book for teaching arithmetic (adding and subtracting) through examples using coins and paper money.

Using Dollar and Sense, Fearon Publishers, 828 Valencia Street, San Francisco, California. (Paper W.B.)

I.L.: junior and senior high school **A.L.:** grades 2–4

A sequel to *Money Makes Sense.* Uses examples from buying, figuring, salary, savings, etc., to reinforce practical multiplication and division concepts.

READING

Adult Education Series, New York: Noble and Noble.

I.L.: senior high school

1. From Words to Stories; 2. How We Live; 3. Your Family and Your Job. (Prepared for adult literacy programs.)

Air Age Books, Chicago, Illinois: Benefic Press.

I.L.: grades 5–8

Two books on the second-grade level, three books on the third-grade level; about rockets, the moon, etc.

American Adventure Series, Chicago, Illinois: Wheeler Publishing Company.

I.L.: junior high school

Three books on second-grade level, three books on third-grade level, four books on fourth-grade level, four books on fifth-grade level, and four books on sixth-grade level. These books are for advanced readers at each level. Teacher's guide for each book. Adventure stories about such men as Kit Carson, Daniel Morgan, Dave Crockett, Buffalo Bill, various Indians, and other historical figures.

Animated Key Cards, New York: Houghton Mifflin Company.

I.L.: primary and elementary

A set of twenty-two plastic cards 4 x 4 inches that give eighteen consonants and four speech consonants in a format that places the letter over a picture that takes the shape of the letter. The student can make the picture appear or disappear by manipulating the card back and forth. The cards would appear to have a high initial interest value because of their novelty. They are designed for developmental work but may be a very useful remedial device for individual work.

Arrow Book Club, Englewood Cliffs, New Jersey: Scholastic Book Service.

I.L.: senior high school **R.L.:** upper half of grade 5

Paperbacks in a number of titles. Some are within the reading and interest levels of better readers.

Bank Street Readers, New York: The Macmillan Company.

I.L.: primary **R.L.:** readiness to grade 3

A series of basic readers designed for use in an urban setting. No special emphasis on the slow learners.

Botel, Morton (ed.). *Interesting Reading Series,* Chicago, Illinois: Follett Publishing Company.

I.L.: intermediate and junior high school **R.L.:** upper half of grades 2 and 3

Nine books in the series. Designed to hold the interest of older students. Basically a supplementary reading series.

Bucky Button Books, Chicago, Illinois: Benefic Press.

Two or more books at each level (pre-primer to grade 3), twelve in all. High interest up to three years above reading level. "Blue collar" family.

City Schools Reading Program, Chicago, Illinois: Follett Publishing Company.

I.L.: primary **R.L.:** primary

A series of books designed for the regular developmental reading program that may interest the intermediate-level slow learner who has not had exposure to materials oriented specifically to describing city life. Described as "multi-cultural" and planned to take advantage of known language patterns. Described as providing shorter stories with more than usual repetition.

Cowboy Sam Series, Chicago, Illinois: Benefic Press.

Three books at each level (pre-primer to grade 3), fifteen in all. Interest level up to three years above reading level. Western adventures.

Dan Frontier Series, Chicago, Illinois: Benefic Press.

Six books, pre-primer through grade 3. High interest stories of adventures on the American Frontier.

The Deep-Sea Adventure Series, San Francisco, California: Harr Wagner Publishing Company.

I.L.: intermediate and junior high school	**R.L.:**
The Sea Hunt	1.8
Treasure under the Sea	2.1
Submarine Rescue	2.4
The Pearl Divers	2.8
Frogmen in Action	3.1
Danger Below	4.4
Whale Hunt	4.7
Rocket Divers	5.0

Developmental Reading Series, Wilkes Barre, Pennsylvania: Lyons and Carnahan.

I.L.: intermediate **R.L.:** primary and intermediate

Regular developmental reading series with Classmate editions for less mature readers.

Dolch Materials, Champaign, Illinois: Garrard Publishing Company.

I.L.: intermediate and junior high school

A large assortment of books and game-like activities that can be used to teach reading. All books have a reduced reading vocabulary.

Elfert and Weinstein. *Achieving Reading Skills,* New York: Globe Book Company.

I.L.: senior high school **R.L.:** grades 4–7

A book designed to improve the reading ability of poor readers in high school.

Feigenbaum. *Effective Reading* and *Successful Reading,* New York: Globe Book Company.

I.L.: senior high school **R.L.:** grades 4–7

Two remedial reading texts designed for use with high school students. Each covers different reading problems.

Fenner and McCrea. *Stories for Fun and Adventure* and *More Stories for Fun and Adventure,* New York: John Day Company.

I.L.: intermediate **R.L.:** not rigidly controlled but approximately third grade

Two anthologies of stories designed specifically to motivate the child in grades 5 and 6 who reads poorly. Stories are light and short.

Functional Basic Reading Series, Pittsburgh, Pennsylvania: Stanwix House, Inc.

I.L.: primary **R.L.:** primary

A developmental reading program of materials created specifically to teach mentally retarded and slow learning pupils to read. Included in the series are reading texts, workbooks, seat work exercises. Supplementary aids and reinforcement activities. Teacher manuals suggest methods for integrating the varied materials into a sequential program of reading instruction.

Getting Started—Communications I; on the Way—Communications II; Full Speed Ahead—Communications III, Chicago, Illinois: Follett Publishing Company. (Paper W.B.)

I.L.: adult **R.L.:** I: grades 0–2
II: grades 3–4
III: grades 5–6

A program to teach literary skills to the adult functional illiterate. Combines reading and writing skills.

Help Yourself to Read, Write, and Spell, New York: Ginn and Company. (Paper Books 1 and 2.)

I.L.: adult **R.L.:** functional vocabulary

Remedial books developed for culturally deprived foreign born. Environmental units used to build 1,200-word functional vocabulary. Teacher handbook available.

Home and Family Life Series, New London, Connecticut: Croft Publishing Company.

I.L.: primary and intermediate **R.L.:** upper half of grade 2

A day with the Brown family: 1. making a good living; 2. the Browns at school; 3. the Browns and their neighbors; 4. supplementary materials for reinforcement with individual readers.

The Jim Forest Readers, San Francisco, California: Harr Wagner Publishing Company.

I.L.: intermediate and junior high school **R.L.:**

Jim Forest and Ranger Don	1.7
Jim Forest and the Bandits	1.9
Jim Forest and the Mystery Hunter	2.2
Jim Forest and Dead Man's Peak	2.6
Jim Forest and the Flood	2.8
Jim Forest and Lone Wolf Gulch	3.1

Learning to Think Series, Red Book, Blue Book, Green Book, Chicago, Illinois: Science Research Associates.

This series gives primary teacher material for young children that combines learning with play. Lesson charts 17 x 22 inches have been prepared as teaching aids for each workbook for use with the class. The series provides direct training for each of the primary mental abilities such as verbal meanings, motor perception, etc.

Lucky Book Club, Englewood Cliffs, New Jersey: Scholastic Book Service.

I.L.: intermediate and junior high school **R.L.:** grades 2–4

Paperbacks in many interest areas. Some may appeal to 13–15 year olds. All are easy to read.

Mixie the Pixie, Special Education Materials, Development Center, 2020 R Street NW, Washington, D.C. (Paper.)

I.L.: primary **R.L.:** primary

A series of illustrated booklets designed to develop basic reading skills. Originally developed in a class for the retarded.

Modern Adventure Stories, New York: Harper & Row Publishers, Inc.

I.L.: intermediate and junior high school **R.L.:** 3.5

A series on a great number of topics. Better readers may enjoy as independent reading.

Morgan Bay Mysteries, San Francisco, California: Harr Wagner Publishing Company.

I.L.: intermediate and junior high school	**R.L.:**
The Mystery of Morgan Castle	2.3
The Mystery of the Marble Angel	2.6
The Mystery of the Midnight Visitor	3.2
The Mystery of the Missing Marlin	3.5
The Mystery of the Musical Ghost	3.5
The Mystery of Monks' Island	3.7
The Mystery of Maurader's Gold	3.9
The Mystery of the Myrmidon's Journey	4.1

Neufeld. *Reading Fundamentals for Teenagers,* New York: John Day Company.

I.L.: junior high school **R.L.:** grades 3 and 4

Corrective reading exercises written with the young teen in mind. Remediation concentrates on comprehension, vocabulary, and word attack. Designed for independent use after being introduced by teacher.

News for You, Box 131, University Station, Syracuse, New York. (One school year, thirty issues.)

A weekly newspaper in easy English for adults. Published October through May.

Pacemaker Story Books, Fearon Publishers, 828 Valencia Street, San Francisco, California. (Paper.)

I.L.: intermediate, junior, and senior high schools **R.L.:** upper half of grade 3

Includes: *Uncle Bill Comes Home, Mystery Cottage, Trail to Adventure, The Strange Artist, Island Adventure, Around the Town.*

Read by Yourself Books, New York: Houghton Mifflin Company.

I.L.: primary and intermediate **R.L.:** upper half of grade 2

May be useful for child who remains on lower reading level for a considerable period.

Reading for a Purpose, Chicago, Illinois: Follett Publishing Company. (Notebook format.)

I.L.: adult **R.L.:** 0–6

A beginning reading program designed to raise undereducated adults to the level of functional literacy.

Reading in High Gear, Chicago, Illinois: Science Research Associates. (Paper W.B.)

I.L.: junior and senior high school **R.L.**: basic developmental reading program

A three-cycle program with four instruction manuals and eight workbooks.

The Reading Motivated Series, San Francisco, California: Harr Wagner Publishing Company.

I.L.: junior high school	**R.L.**:
Desert Treasure	4.5
The Mysterious Swamp Rider	4.7
The Secret of Lonesome Valley	4.7
Adventures in Apacheland	5.3

Reading Skill Builders, Pleasantville, New York: Reader's Digest Educational Department. (Paper.)

I.L.: intermediate, junior, and senior high schools **R.L.**: grades 2–8, 2–5

Simple, interesting stories with reinforcement material. Three books at each grade level. Teacher manual available for each grade level. Also Adult Education Readers I–II. (Readers are not monthly periodicals.)

Scope, Englewood Cliffs, New Jersey: Scholastic Book Service.

I.L.: junior and senior high school **R.L.**: not given

A weekly magazine designed to interest the "hard to reach" students. Advertised as exciting and easy to read. Stresses social and vocational development.

S.R.A. *Pilot Library,* Chicago, Illinois: Science Research Associates. (Paper; three libraries, seventy-two books in each.)

I.L.: grades 4, 6, 8, and 9 **R.L.**: 2–7, 4–9, and 5–12

A set of materials developed for use with the S.R.A. Reading Laboratory. Short selection excerpted from well-known literature. Presented as a way to supply supplementary reading material for those who need practice.

S.R.A. *Reading Laboratories,* Chicago, Illinois: Science Research Associates. (Card format.)

I.L.: 1–12 **R.L.**: 1–12

A carefully planned developmental reading program that starts the student at his level and gradually brings him upward through a series of specific reading skill builders. Planned for individual student use. Not designed specifically for slow learners but reported as used by them in the literature.

Study Exercises for Developing Reading Skills, River Forest, Illinois: Laidlaw Brothers. (Paper W.B.)

I.L.: intermediate to senior high school **R.L.:** intermediate

A series of workbooks designed to help a number of basic reading skills. Not designed specifically for the slow learner.

System for Success, Books 1 and 2, Chicago, Illinois: Follett Publishing Company. (Paper W.B.)

I.L.: high school or adult

Several books in an expanding series designed to give the semiliterate adult a basic education. Uses phonics as its basic approach.

Teen-age Book Club, Englewood Cliffs, New Jersey: Scholastic Book Service.

I.L.: junior and senior high school **R.L.:** upper half of grade 4

Paperback selections.

Teen-age Tales, New York: D. C. Heath and Company.

I.L.: high school **R.L.:** upper half of grade 4

Teen-age activities and problems. Reader has opportunity for self-evaluation. About eight volumes.

Wildlife Adventure Series, San Francisco, California: Harr Wagner Publishing Company.

I.L.: upper intermediate, junior high school	**R.L.:**
Gatie the Alligator	4.1
Sleeky the Otter	4.4
Skipper the Dolphin	4.6
Tawny the Mountain Lion	4.8
Bounder the Jackrabbit	5.0
Thor the Moose	5.1
Ruff the Wolf	5.3
Arctos the Grizzly	5.5

SCIENCE

What Is It Series, Chicago, Illinois: Benefic Press.

R.L.: grades 1–6 **I.L.:** grades 1–6

Science series; thirty books in all; filmstrips may be ordered for the above books.

SOCIAL AND VOCATIONAL DEVELOPMENT

Better Living, Gary D. Lawson, 9488 Sara Street, Elk Grove, California. (Paper W.B.)

I.L.: high school **R.L.:** upper half of grade 4

Covers moral education and education for marriage and parenthood.

Driver Training Workbook Program, R. W. Parkinson, 704 Manford Drive, Urbana, Illinois.

A book of units in traffic safety and driving rules. Originally developed for use in classes for the mentally retarded.

Finding Your Job, Finney Company, 3350 Corham Avenue, Minneapolis, Minnesota. (Paper.)

I.L.: high school **R.L.:** upper half of grade 4

Three units, five volumes per unit. A series of brief job descriptions originally developed for use in classes for the mentally retarded. Should be used with results of a job survey in the local area.

I Want a Driver's License, R. W. Parkinson, 704 Manford Drive, Urbana, Illinois. (Paper W.B.)

I.L.: high school **R.L.:** grade 4

Originally developed for use in classes for mentally retarded. Must be adapted to conform to local law. Probably best used as a teacher's guide.

Keyboard Town, R. W. Parkinson, 704 Manford Drive, Urbana, Illinois. (Paper.)

I.L.: intermediate and junior high school

Typing program. See study by Karnes, et al., *Exceptional Children*, 31: 27 (September, 1964). Program developed for mentally retarded.

Manpower Development and Training Program, Washington, D.C.: U.S. Government Printing Office. (Paper.)

I.L.: high school **R.L.:** teacher's use

Suggested Training Programs: Hotel and Motel Housekeeping Aide; Forestry Aide; Clothing Maintenance Specialist; Companion to an Elderly Person; Family Dinner Service Specialist; Homemaker's Assistant; Landscape Aide; Supervised Food Service Worker. A series of booklets prepared for use in home economics and vocational education, though not designed specifically for the retarded.

Newspaper Reading. Gary D. Lawson, 9488 Sara Street, Elk Grove, California. (Paper W.B.)

I.L.: high school **R.L.:** grade 4

Provides a systematic approach to teaching the use of a newspaper; originally developed for the mentally retarded.

Occupational Education, Eye Gate House, 146–01 Archer Avenue, Jamaica, New York.

I.L.: high school

Nine filmstrips to the set. Deals with various jobs and some specific vocational adjustment skills; originally developed for use with the mentally retarded.

Road Signs, Fern Tripp, 2035 East Sierra Way, Dinuba, California.

I.L.: junior and senior high school

120 signs in authentic shapes. Actual color used. An inexpensive way to teach road signs. May be used for review of driver's test. Signs should be used only after checking state traffic laws. Some signs may not apply.

New Rochester Occupational Reading Series, Chicago, Illinois: Science Research Associates. (Paper W.B. and hard text.)

I.L.: junior and senior high school **R.L.:** grades 2, 3, and 4; grades 4 and 5 Standardized Reading Texts

Revision of the Rochester workbooks that have enjoyed popularity for a good number of years. Includes a teacher's guide; this series concentrates on general approach to prevocational education. Series entitled "The Job Ahead." Individual sections on: 1. Starting work; 2. On the job; 3. Keeping the job; 4. Working for the city; 5. Time out for leisure. Stories and materials are separate; stories are hard bound (one book for each level). Teacher's guide includes master lists of useful vocational words. Also lists guidance topics.

Snip, Clip, and Stitch, R. W. Parkinson, 704 Manford Drive, Urbana, Illinois. (Paper W.B.)

I.L.: junior and senior high school

A course on clothing construction for the educable mentally retarded. Many illustrations supplement the text on introductory sewing techniques. The teacher's manual is designed so that the course can be taught by a person with little previous training in home economics.

Teenagers Prepare for Work, Mrs. Esther Carson, 18623 Lake Chabot Road, Castro Valley, California. (Paper W.B.)

I.L.: high school **R.L.:** grade 4

Books I and II: Workbooks around general prevocational situations. Developed for use in classes for the mentally retarded.

Turner-Livingston Communication Series, Chicago, Illinois: Follett Publishing Company. (Paper W.B.)

I.L.: high school **R.L.:** grades 6–7

The Television You Watch
The Language You Speak
The Newspaper You Read
The Letters You Write
The Movies You See
The Phone Calls You Make

A series of workbooks designed to build reading skills while making the student more aware of his environment.

Turner-Livingston Reading Series, Chicago, Illinois: Follett Publishing Company. (Paper W.B.)

I.L.: high school **R.L.:** grades 5–6

The Family You Belong To
The Money You Spend
The Friends You Make
The Town You Live In
The Jobs You Get
The Person You Are

A series of booklets designed to help the poor achiever get ready for life. Integrates several subjects under one interest area. Contains stories that have accompanying drills and quizzes.

Understanding the Automobile, Reading for a Purpose Specimen Set, Chicago, Illinois: Follett Publishing Company. (Paper W.B.)

I.L.: senior high school **R.L.:** grades 6–7

Breaks the automobile into nine basic systems. Provides precise information on each. Includes many drawings and self-testing exercises.

Vocational Reading Series, Chicago, Illinois: Follett Publishing Company. (Paper W.B.)

I.L.: senior high school **R.L.:** grades 4–6

The Millers and Willie B, Butcher, Baker, Chef
John Leveron, Auto Mechanic
The Delso Sisters, Beauticians
Marie Perrone, Practical Nurse

At present this series consists of four booklets. All are designed to improve language skills and to introduce students to jobs that may provide careers for them.

SOCIAL STUDIES

Accent Education Series, Chicago, Illinois: Follett Publishing Company. (Paper W.B.)

I.L.: adult and young adult **R.L.:** grades 3–4

A series of six booklets designed to stimulate discussion on basic social skills and concepts. Format will accommodate nonreaders.

Foundations of Citizenship, Books I and II, Frank E. Richards, 215 Church Street, Phoenix, New York. (Paper W.B.)

I.L.: senior high school **R.L.:** varies

Volume 1: After School Is Out
Volume 2: Al Looks for a Job
Volume 3: On the Job

A series on social adjustment as it relates to vocational success. Originally written for the mentally retarded.

Frontiers of American Books, Chicago, Illinois: Children's Press, Inc.

I.L.: junior high school **R.L.:** upper half of grade 3

A series of thirteen titles with a teacher's guide. May be useful as supplementary material for social studies.

Modified History of the United States, Ardelle Manning Productions, Palo Alto, California.

Prepared for use with the secondary level educable mentally retarded student. Extends from early explorers to World War II. Text is illustrated with black and white drawings. Each chapter includes list of new terms and followup questions to test knowledge gained.

Schwartz and O'Connor. *Exploring American History,* New York: Globe Book Company.

I.L.: senior high school **R.L.:** grade 5.5

A book covering regular American history curriculum that was written specifically for slow learners. Vocabulary controlled. Includes student exercises. Teacher's manual available.

———. *Exploring a Changing World,* New York: Globe Book Company.

I.L.: senior high school **R.L.:** grades 5–6

A geography text designed specifically for slow learners in the secondary school. Includes a number of pictures, maps, and charts.

The Story of America, River Forest, Illinois: Laidlaw Brothers.

I.L.: junior high school **R.L.:** "low level"

An American history text prepared for the culturally disadvantaged.

Study Lessons in Our Nation's History, Chicago, Illinois: Follett Publishing Company. (Paper W.B.)

I.L.: elementary and junior high school **R.L.:** grades 4–7

Eight booklets in the set. Advertised as having been developed specifically for use by slow learners in social studies. Emphasis on controlled reading.

Target Series, Ebensburg, Pennsylvania: Mafex Association. (Paper.)

I.L.: junior and senior high school **R.L.:** grade 4

A series of student texts, workbooks, and teacher's guides divided into three phases: (1) citizenship; (2) employment; (3) family living and business. Posters available for employment phases. Workbook for family phases emphasizes budgeting. In all phases ideas are developed through interesting stories designed to appeal to teenagers.

World History Study Lessons, Chicago, Illinois: Follett Publishing Company. (Paper W.B.)

I.L.: senior high school **R.L.:** grades 6–8

Nine booklets in a set. Advertised as being developed for slow learners. Uses systematic approach.

Your and Your World, Fearon Publishers, 828 Valencia Street, San Francisco, California. (Paper W.B.)

A self-contained workbook on social studies. Reading material is based on the Stone revision of the Dale list of 769 easy words. Teacher's guide.

APPENDIX B

A Basic Reference Library for Teachers Who Work with Slow Learners

A brief annotated bibliography of books often found in the personal collections of teachers who have an interest in slow learning

American Educational Research Association. "Education for Socially Disadvantaged Children," *Review of Educational Research,* 25:373–442 (December, 1965).

This review is useful background material for teachers who work with slow learners from disadvantaged areas. Most of the research reported has been conducted since 1960, although a number of older preliminary or "classic" studies are included to provide a frame of reference to more recent research. Some of the specific topics included are: Characteristics of Socially Disadvantaged Children; Language Development in Socially Disadvantaged Children; and Programs and Practices in Compensatory Education for the Disadvantaged.

Abraham, Willard. *The Slow Learner.* New York: The Center for Applied Research in Education, 1964. 113 pp.

This book presents a general coverage of the problem of slow learning. An interesting departure from the usual content is the author's consideration of the gifted slow learner. Attention is given to the topic, "The Parents and the Community." Approximately twenty-five pages are devoted to various school concerns. Three appendices include a case study and two descriptions of current programs for slow learners in Arizona. The book contains an eight-page bibliography of books and articles devoted to slow learning and a number of other related topics.

Baber, Eric (compiler). *Programs for the Educationally Disadvantaged.* U.S. Department of Health, Education, and Welfare, Bulletin 1963, No. 17.

Washington, D.C.: U.S. Government Printing Office, 1963. 105 pp.

This book resulted from a 1962 conference on teaching educationally disadvantaged children. The teacher of slow learners will be interested in the descriptions of school programs in various cities throughout the country. There are several reports of attempts to formulate curriculum designs that would appear to be especially suited to the slower students.

Bloom, Benjamin S. *Compensatory Education for Cultural Deprivation.* New York: Holt, Rinehart and Winston, 1965. 179 pp.

This book is the report of the 1964 research conference on cultural deprivation. The book contains a rather complete annotated bibliography that should assist teachers in understanding the intellectual development of culturally deprived slow learners. A number of other background ideas are also available from this publication.

Brown, Eleanor B. *The Slow Learner in Business Education. A Selected Bibliography.* Kent, Ohio: Kent State University, Bureau of Economic and Business Research, 1964. 22 pp.

This is an un-numbered, nonannotated bibliography that includes a considerable number of references to the retarded and other exceptional groups in addition to slow learners. References are included without apparent consideration of their timeliness. No introductory material is included. One of the very few specialized bibliographies available.

Brown, Kenneth E., and Theodore L. Abell. *Analysis of Research in the Teaching of Mathematics.* Washington, D.C.: U.S. Government Printing Office, 1965. 96 pp.

This is a useful compilation of general research activity in mathematics education. It is the sixth in a series of such publications, and the earlier editions are required if the teacher is to have a complete record of research. This publication covers the years 1961–1962. It lists general research activity including doctoral dissertations plus appropriate cooperative research projects that were complete at time of publication.

Brueckner, Leo J., and Guy L. Bond. *The Diagnosis and Treatment of Learning Difficulties.* New York: Appleton-Century-Crofts, 1955. 424 pp.

The authors outline methods of making a complete educational diagnosis, then proceed to suggest remedial techniques based on an individual diagnostic plan. Attention is given to reading, arithmetic, language, spelling, and handwriting. The book is not written for slow learners but should assist the teacher in arriving at a balanced diagnostic picture of their learning difficulties.

Burchill, George W. *Work Study Programs for Alienated Youth.* Chicago: Science Research Associated, 1962. 265 pp.

This book presents brief case histories of work-study programs that have been designed specifically to meet the vocational training needs of various types of alienated youth. The Rochester, New York, program for slow learners is described in detail. A discussion of the over-all problem of alienation and of the specific elements that constitute a work-study program are included.

Cohen, Dorothy H., and Virginia Stern. *Observing and Recording the Behavior of Young Children.* New York: Teachers College Press, 1958. 86 pp.

This book describes techniques that may prove helpful to the teacher who is attempting to identify those younger students who require special help. The book is designed to make everyday observations more systematic and thus more helpful.

Cohen, Julius, Robert J. Gregory, and John W. Pelosi. *Vocational Rehabilitation and the Socially Disabled.* Syracuse, New York: The Syracuse University Press, 1966. 69 pp.

This report on the 1965 conference, "Rehabilitation Counseling and the Poverty Field," provides insight into a rapidly developing field that may at some future time play a major role in the life planning of slow learners.

Conant, James B. *Slums and Suburbs.* New York: McGraw-Hill, 1961. 200 pp.

This book presents an over-all view of the sharp contrasts that exist between urban and suburban schools. Particular emphasis is placed on the non-college-bound student. Suggestions for curriculum and administrative changes are included.

Crow, Lester D., Walter I. Murray, and Hugh H. Smythe. *Educating the Culturally Disadvantaged Child.* New York: David McKay, 1966. 306 pp.

This book is designed to give teachers an over-view of who the disadvantaged child is, what his problems are, and how he should be approached in school. Coverage is given to a number of disadvantaged groups in addition to Negro children in urban slums. Each chapter includes a series of problems designed to provoke discussion. Teacher preparation is a major topic. Descriptions of various programs for the disadvantaged occupy approximately one-half of the publication. This is not a book of readings.

Featherstone, William. *Teaching the Slow Learner,* rev. ed., New York: Teachers College Press, 1951. 118 pp.

This book contains many nuggets of practical advice that have not been surpassed in the rather long period of time since its publication. Many of its teaching suggestions are still relevant. The book presents a general over-view of slow learning.

Frost, Joe L., and Glenn R. Hawkes. *The Disadvantaged Child.* New York: Houghton Mifflin Co., 1966. 445 pp.

This book is a collection of readings culled from professional magazines. The material is useful as background to understanding the problems of the culturally deprived slow learner. The section on intelligence will be of particular interest to teachers of slower students.

Goldberg, Miriam, A. Harry Passow, and Joseph Justman. *The Effects of Ability Grouping.* New York: Teachers College Press, 1966. 254 pp.

This report results from a study of over 2,000 public school children who were grouped according to ability. The report reviews relevant research, sets up certain hypotheses, and describes the field study in which they were tested. The book has important implications for administering programs for slow learners.

Hilgard, Ernest R. (ed.). *Theories of Learning and Instruction,* National Society for the Study of Education, Sixty-third Yearbook, Part Two, Chicago: University of Chicago Press, 1964. 430 pp.

This book should prove useful to the teacher who feels that his grasp of learning theory is rather weak. It presents a great deal of thought-provoking material.

Howitt, Lillian C. *Creative Techniques for Teaching the Slow Learner.* New York: Teachers Practical Press, 1964. 64 pp.

This book presents the classroom teacher with some practical ideas. There is little focus on the theoretical. The main emphasis is on English and social studies instruction. Sample lessons, suggested games, and similar materials are included.

Hunt, DeWitt. *Work Experience Education Programs in American Secondary Schools,* Bulletin, 1957, No. 5, Washington, D.C.: U.S. Government Printing Office, 1957. 94 pp.

This book presents a rather complete over-view of the specific elements that should be included in a successful work-study program. The material presented would seem to have particular value for those professionals who are contemplating the establishment of a school work-study program for slow learners.

Jewett, Arno, and J. Dan Jull. *Teaching Rapid and Slow Learners in High School,* Bulletin, 1954, No. 5, Washington, D.C.: U.S. Government Printing Office, 1954. 97 pp.

This book is obsolete in terms of its statistics, but it should provide the secondary school teacher with some guidelines that will prove of value in developing a new program.

Jewett, Arno, Joseph Mersand, and Doris V. Gunderson (eds.). *Improving English Skills of Culturally Different Youth in Large Cities.* Washington, D.C.: U.S. Government Printing Office, 1964. 216 pp.

This booklet is not designed for use with slow learners, but it does concentrate on the problem of communication that is so central to the slower child. The various contributors touch on a number of topics including research, improving language skills, and teacher qualifications and training. Descriptions of a number of programs are included.

Johnson, G. Orville. *Education for the Slow Learners*. Englewood Cliffs, New Jersey: Prentice-Hall, 1963. 33 pp.

This book is a comprehensive review of the problem of slow learning and its educational treatment.

Kephart, Newell C. *The Slow Learner in the Classroom*. Columbus, Ohio: Charles R. Merrill, 1960. 292 pp.

The term "slow learner" is used here in a descriptive sense. The book describes a number of activities that can be used to diagnose and correct the lack of psycho-motor development in the young child.

Kirk, Samuel A. *Teaching Reading to Slow Learning Children*. Boston: Houghton Mifflin, 1940. 225 pp.

The focus of the book is the mentally retarded child. A chapter is devoted to slow learners who are described as "dull normal." Except for the fact that its appendices are out of date, this book is still one of the standard texts in its field.

Liebherr, Harold G., and Glen E. Peterson (eds.). *The Teacher and BSCS Special Materials*. Boulder, Colorado: Biological Sciences Curriculum Study, 1966. 70 pp.

This booklet describes the biological sciences project and suggests implications of the project for the academically unsuccessful student. Attention is given to administrative and instructional procedures. Suggestions for preparing teachers to use the special materials also are included.

Otto, Wayne, and Richard A. McMenemy. *Corrective and Remedial Teaching*. Boston: Houghton Mifflin Co., 1966. 377 pp.

This book is specifically oriented toward the underachiever but contains a number of diagnostic and teaching suggestions that might be helpful in working with slow learners.

Passow, A. Harry (ed.). *Intellectual Development: Another Look*. Washington, D.C., A.S.C.D., 1964. 119 pp

This book should prove valuable to the teacher who is interested in learning more about how children learn. The chapter on intellectual development in early childhood education has definite implications for the diagnosis and education of slow learners.

Potter, Mary, and Virgil Mallory. *Education in Mathematics for the Slow Learner*. Washington, D.C.: National Council of Teachers of Mathematics, 1958. 36 pp.

The authors review the characteristics of slow learners, mention important elements to be included in instructional planning, and present various materials that they feel will be helpful. A general bibliography is included. Unfortunately, the book's usefulness is somewhat impaired by its age.

Riessman, Frank. *The Culturally Deprived Child.* New York: Harper & Row, 1962. 140 pp.

This book presents rather completely one of the several current views of the problem of cultural deprivation. It should help the teacher of slow learners to become more sensitive to his students' needs.

Rosenbloom, Paul C. (ed.). *C.A.M.P. Project Conference Report.* Pella, Iowa: Central College Press, 1966. 53 pp.

This report of a 1966 conference on special mathematical programs for low achievers in grades 7 through 9 reviews the problems of low achievement in mathematics and reports on a number of experimental programs.

Stratemeyer, Florence B., et al. *Developing a Curriculum for Modern Living.* New York: Teachers College Press, 1957. 740 pp.

This book sets forth the philosophy and structure of the persistent life-situations approach to curriculum building, an approach that is often reflected in programs for slow learners.

Ullmann, Charles A. *Identification of Maladjusted School Children,* Public Health Monograph No. 7. Washington, D.C.: U.S. Government Printing Office, 1957. 41 pp.

A report on a study of three different approaches to identifying students whose mental and/or emotional characteristics are such that they should receive psychological assistance. It should be of interest to the teacher of slow learners who is interested in preventing behavior problems.

United States Department of Health, Education, and Welfare—Manpower Development and Training Program. *Educationally Deficient Adults.* Washington, D.C.: U.S. Government Printing Office, 1965. 60 pp.

This descriptive study of educationally deficient adults points up the need for stronger programs designed to meet the special needs of children who are still in school.

University of the State of New York. *Suggestions for Teaching Business Pupils of Different Ability Levels—with Special Emphasis on Pupils Experiencing Difficulty.* Albany, New York: Bureau of Business and Distributive Education, State Education Department, 1964. 44 pp.

This is a general guide for adapting instruction in business subjects. A special bibliography, arranged by business subjects, is included.

Woodby, Lauren G. *The Low Achiever in Mathematics.* Washington, D.C.: U.S. Government Printing Office, 1965. 96 pp.

This report of a 1964 conference on improving mathematics instruction deals with the student who cannot profit from a conventional mathematics program. It provides a good background for teachers of slow learners. The report includes descriptions of several experimental programs.

Wellington, Charles Burleigh, and Jean Wellington. *The Underachiever—Challenges and Guidelines.* Chicago: Rand McNally, 1965. 122 pp.

This book provides the teacher of slow learners with a quick overview of the problem of underachievement that is so often confused with the problem of slow learning.

Bibliography

GENERAL REFERENCES

1. Abraham, Willard. "A Variety of Ideas Pertinent to the Slow Learner," *Education,* 81:352–355 (February, 1961).

2. ———. *The Slow Learner.* New York: The Center for Applied Research in Education, Inc., 1964. 113 pp.

3. Almy, Millie. "New Views on Intellectual Development in Early Childhood Education," *Intellectual Development: Another Look,* A. Harry Passow (ed.), Washington, D.C.: The Association for Curriculum Development, 1964. 119 pp.

4. American Association on Mental Deficiency. *A Manual on Terminology and Classification in Mental Retardation,* monograph supplement, American Association on Mental Deficiency, No. 64, September, 1959. 111 pp.

5. Anderson, Robert, Ellis A. Hagstrom, and Wade M. Robinson. "Team Teaching in an Elementary School," *School Review,* 68:71–84 (Spring, 1960).

6. Baarstad, David L. "A Resource Room for the Educationally Handicapped Pupil," *California Education,* 3:14–15 (December, 1965).

7. Bartlett, Claude J., and Alfred A. Baumeister. "Prediction of Classroom Discipline Problems," *Exceptional Children,* 27:216–220 (December, 1960).

8. Barwick, Janice M., and George Arbuckle. "A Study of the Relationship Between Parental Acceptance and the Academic Achievement of Adolescents," *Journal of Educational Research,* 56:148–151 (November, 1962).

9. Becken, Elliott D. "Revised Instructional Program for 'Slow Learners' to Improve Their Job Placement Opportunities: A Three Phase

Study," *Progress Report,* Medford, Oregon, March, 1966. 15 pp. with unpaged appendices. Mimeographed.

10. Beier, Delton C. "Behavioral Disturbances in the Mentally Retarded," *Mental Retardation,* Harvey A. Stevens and Rick Heber (eds.), Chicago: Chicago University Press, 1964. 502 pp.

11. Bolzau, E. L., and E. L. Keltz. "What Shall We Do for the Slow Learner?" *American School Board Journal,* 133:37–38 (November, 1956).

12. Brueckner, Leo J., and Guy L. Bond. *The Diagnosis and Treatment of Learning Difficulties.* New York: Appleton-Century-Crofts, 1955. 424 pp.

13. Brunda, Huberta S. "Slow Learner in the Regular Classroom," *School and Community,* 48:28–37 (October, 1961).

14. Bruner, Jerome (ed.). *Learning about Learning.* Washington, D.C.: Government Printing Office, 1966. 276 pp.

15. Chidley, Nadine. "Special Education for the Slow Learner," *Canadian Education and Research Digest,* 3:204–215 (September, 1963).

16. Cirone, Claire, and Patricia Emerson. "The Slow Learner in a New Setting: A Continuous Progress Program," *New York State Education,* 53:19–22 (January, 1966).

17. Cohen, Julius S. *Vocational Rehabilitation and the Socially Disabled.* Syracuse, New York: Syracuse University Press, 1966. 86 pp.

18. Conant, James B. *Slums and Suburbs.* New York: McGraw-Hill, 1961. 200 pp.

19. Corcoran, Eileen L. "Rx for the Slow Learner," *New York State Education,* 52:15–17 (May, 1965).

20. Corey, Stephen M., and Virgil E. Herrick. "The Developmental Tasks of Children and Young People," *The Child,* Jerome Seidman (ed.), New York: Holt, Rinehart, and Winston, 1957. 674 pp.

21. Davey, Edward J. "The Supervisor's Role in Creating a Sound Nonacademic Program," *Clearing House,* 37:368–372 (February, 1963).

22. Dean, Stuart E. "Team Teaching: A Review," *School Life,* 44:5–8 (September, 1961).

23. Derthick, Lawrence. "Education of the Slow Learners," *Education,* 81:336–337 (February, 1961).

24. Dolmatch, Theodore B., and Albert J. Mazurkiewicz. "The Promise of i.t.a. Is a Delusion: No!" *Phi Delta Kappan,* 47:550–552 (June, 1966).

25. Downing, John A. *The Initial Teaching Alphabet.* New York: The Macmillan Company, 1964. 150 pp.

26. ———. *The Initial Teaching Alphabet Reading Experiment.* Chicago: Scott Foresman, 1965. 144 pp.

27. Drummond, Harold D. "Team Teaching: An Assessment," *Educational Leadership,* 19:160–165 (December, 1961).

28. Dulles, Robert J. "The Myth of Underachievement," *Journal of Educational Sociology,* 35:121–122 (November, 1961).

29. Easterday, Kenneth E. "Technique for Low Achievers," *Mathematics Teacher,* 58:519–521 (October, 1965).

30. Fisher, J. Sherrick. "Significance of the I.Q.," *Phi Delta Kappan,* 40:258–259 (March, 1959).

31. Frain, Thomas J. *Administrative and Instructional Provisions for Rapid and Slow Learners in Catholic Secondary Schools.* Washington, D.C.: The Catholic University of America Press, 1956. 143 pp.

32. French, Joseph. "Significance of the Deviation I.Q. for Exceptional Children," *Phi Delta Kappan,* 40:325 (May, 1959).

33. Frostig, Marianne, and David Horne. *The Frostig Program for the Development of Visual Perception.* Chicago: Follett Publishing Co., 1964. 168 pp.

34. Gallagher, James J., and James W. Moss. "New Concepts of Intelligence and Their Effect on Exceptional Children," *Exceptional Children,* 30:1–5 (September, 1963).

35. Gilhooly, William B. "The Promise of i.t.a. Is a Delusion: Yes!" *Phi Delta Kappan,* 47:545–550 (June, 1966).

36. Glaser, Robert (ed.). *Teaching Machines and Programmed Learning II: Data and Directions.* Washington, D.C.: Department of Audiovisual Instruction, National Education Association, 1965. 832 pp.

37. Goldstein, Herbert. "New Directions for the Slow Learner," *Education,* 81:348–351 (February, 1961).

38. ——— and Edith Levitt. *A Reading Readiness Program for the Mentally Retarded,* Urbana, Illinois: R. W. Parkinson and Associates, 1963. 24 pp.

39. Goodlad, John I. "Some Effects of Promotion and Non-Promotion upon the Social and Personal Adjustment of Children," *Journal of Experimental Education,* 22:301–328 (June, 1954).

40. Gowan, John Curtis. "Dynamics of the Underachievement of Gifted Students," *Exceptional Children,* 24:98–101 (November, 1957).

41. Gray, G. "Educational Technology and the Individual Student," *Phi Delta Kappan,* 46:6–8 (September, 1964).

42. Guggenheim, Fred, and Corinne Guggenheim (eds.). *New Frontiers in Education.* New York: Grune and Stratton, 1966. 310 pp.

43. Havighurst, Robert J. "Dealing with Problem Youth," *Nation's Schools,* 61:43–50 (May, 1958).

44. Hillson, Maurie. "Nongraded Schools: Organizational Design for Elementary Education," in *Change and Innovation in Elementary School Organization,* Maurie Hillson and Ramona Karlson (eds.), New York: Holt, Rinehart, and Winston, 1965. 387 pp.

45. ——— and Ramona Karlson (eds.). *Change and Innovation in Elementary School Organization.* New York: Holt, Rinehart, and Winston, 1965. 387 pp.

46. Holland, Howard, and Armand J. Galfo. *An Analysis of Research Concerning Class Size.* Richmond, Virginia: Division of Research, State Department, 1964. 21 pp.

47. Initial Teaching Alphabet Publications. "i.t.a.: Special Education," *i.t.a. Bulletin,* 3:10–14 (Fall, 1965).

48. Johnson, G. Orville. *Education for the Slow Learners.* Englewood Cliffs, New Jersey: Prentice-Hall, 1963. 330 pp.

49. ———. "Slow Learner: the Forgotten Student in Today's High School," *High School Journal,* 48:147–151 (December, 1964).

50. Karnes, Merle B. "The Slow Learner—Administrative Plans that Help," *National Education Association Journal,* 48:147–151 (December, 1964).

51. ———. "Progress Report: A Prevocational Curriculum and Services Designed to Rehabilitate Slow Learners," Project RD-1075-P, Champaign Community Schools, Unit IV, February, 1964. Unpaged, mimeographed.

52. Kirk, Samuel A. *Early Education of the Mentally Retarded.* Urbana, Illinois: University of Illinois Press, 1958. 216 pp.

53. ———. "Research in Education," *Mental Retardation—A Review of Research,* Harvey A. Stevens and Rick Heber (eds.), Chicago: University of Chicago Press, 1964. 502 pp.

54. Klein, Erwin J. "Cooperative Occupational Training Program; A Taste of Success for Low I.Q. Students," *Bulletin of the National Association of Secondary School Principals,* 50:64–69 (March, 1966).

55. Kvaraceus, William. "The Behavioral Deviate in the Secondary School," *Phi Delta Kappan,* 40:102–104 (November, 1958).

56. Liddle, Gordon, and Dale Long. "Experimental Room for Slow Learners," *Elementary School Journal,* 59:143–146 (December, 1958).

57. Liggett, Margaret, and Beulah Sellers. "They Can Learn . . . If Taught," *Journal of Home Economics,* 54:357–360 (May, 1962).

58. Lodato, Francis J., and Martin A. Sokoloff. "Group Counseling for Slow Learners," *Journal of Counseling Psychology,* 10:95–96 (September, 1963).

59. Loretan, Joseph O. "The Decline and Fall of Group Intelligence Testing," *Teachers College Record,* 67:10–17 (October, 1965).

60. Mackie, Romaine P. "Spotlighting Advances in Special Education," *Exceptional Children,* 32:77–81 (October, 1965).

61. Mahan, Thomas W. (Jr.). "Slow Learner: Fact or Excuse," *School Review,* 73:77–78 (Summer, 1965).

62. Matthews, Charles V., and Frank D. Sorenson. "An Educational Program for Slow Learners in Grades 7 through 12," Carbondale, Illinois: Southern Illinois University, December, 1964. 25 pp. Mimeographed.

63. Medina Central School. "The Prevocational Program in Grades 7–12 of Medina Central Schools," fifth progress report, Medina, New York, February, 1965. 28 pp. Mimeographed.

64. Morgenstern, Anne. *Grouping in the Elementary School.* New York: Pitman Publishing Company, 1966. 118 pp.

65. National Education Association, Department of Home Economics. *The Slow Learner in Homemaking Education,* Department of Home Economics Topics, No. 10, Washington, D.C.: The Department (March, 1959). 15 pp.

66. Neill, Alexander S. "A Radical Approach to Child Rearing," *Summerhill,* New York: Hart Publishing Co., Inc., 1960. 392 pp.

67. Orr, David, and Herbert L. Friedman. *A Summary of Time Compressed Speech Research of the American Institutes for Research,* no date. 3 pp. Mimeographed.

68. Otto, Wayne, and Richard A. McMenemy. *Corrective and Remedial Teaching.* Boston: Houghton Mifflin & Co., 1966. 377 pp.

69. Phillips, Jack. "A C-Core Program Pays Off," *Clearing House,* 40:262–264 (January, 1966).

70. Reid, Ann. "Are Special Classes for Slow Learners Worthwhile?" *Clearing House,* 32:553–555 (May, 1958).

71. Reid, James M. "Six Years of P I: A Summing Up," *Programmed Instruction,* 3:10–11 (May, 1964).

72. Reiner, William B. "Provision for the Slow Learner," *Science Teacher,* 28:33–35 (November, 1961).

73. Rochester, Minnesota, Public Schools. "Help for the Slow Learner," summary report of workshop, August 27, 1965, Rochester, Minnesota: The Public Schools, 1966. 45 pp. Mimeographed.

74. Shaplin, Judson T. "Team Teaching and the Curriculum," in *Innovation and Experiment in Modern Education,* Arthur E. Traxler (ed.), Washington, D.C.: American Council on Education, 1965. 159 pp.

75. Sorensen, Mourits A. "Counseling Marginal Students on Classroom Behavior," *Personnel and Guidance Journal,* 40:811–813 (May, 1962).

76. Sotis, James N. "What Can We Do About the Slow Learner? A Terminal Certificate Plan," *New York State Education,* 51:18–19 (February, 1964).

77. Strang, Ruth. "Teaching Slow-Learning Children in Elementary School," *Education,* 81:338–340 (February, 1961).

78. Strom, Robert D. "Realistic Curriculum for the Predictive Dropout," *Clearing House,* 39:101–109 (October, 1964).

79. Terman, Lewis N., and Maud Merrill. *Measuring Intelligence.* Cambridge, Massachusetts: The Riverside Press, 1937. 461 pp.

80. Thurston, John R. "Too Close to Normalcy," *Clearing House,* 38:296–298 (January, 1964).

81. Traxler, Arthur E. (ed.). *Innovation and Experiment in Modern Education.* Washington, D.C.: American Council on Education, 1965. 159 pp.

82. U.S. Department of Health, Education and Welfare, Office of Education. *Teaching Rapid and Slow Learners in High Schools,* Bulletin Number 5, Government Printing Office, 1954. 97 pp.

83. Utley, Ishmel. "The Slow Learner in the Secondary School," *Education,* 81:341–345 (February, 1961).

84. Varner, Glenn F. "Youth with Non-academic Abilities and/or Interests: What Are Secondary Schools Doing to Provide for Youth with Non-academic Abilities and/or Interests?" *National Association of Secondary Schools Bulletin,* 39:294–297 (April, 1955).

85. Wellington, C. Burleigh, and Jean Wellington: *The Underachiever: Challenges and Guidelines.* Chicago: Rand, McNally, 1965. 122 pp.

86. Wenrich, Ralph C. "Secondary Education for the Academically Untalented," *School and Society,* 92:259 (September, 1964).

87. West, Jeff. "Grouping Slow Learners," *Education*, 81:345–347 (February, 1961).

88. Witty, Paul. "Needs of Slow Learning Pupils," *Education*, 81:331–335 (February, 1961).

89. Zeitz, F. "i.t.a. and the Below-Average Child; with Reply by A. Mazurkiewicz and Rejoinder," *Reading Teacher*, 19:515–518 (April, 1966).

CHARACTERIZATION

90. Barber, Robert W. "My Slow Students are Personality Problems," *Clearing House*, 29:203–206 (December, 1954).

91. Bloom, Benjamin S. *Stability and Change in Human Characteristics.* New York: John Wiley & Sons, Inc., 1964. 237 pp.

92. Boger, James H. "An Experimental Study of the Effects of Perceptual Training on Group I.Q. Scores of Elementary Pupils in Rural Ungraded Schools," *Journal of Educational Research*, 46:43–53 (January, 1952).

93. Cobb, Marion M. "Slow Learners in Action," *High Points*, 44:59–66 (November, 1962).

94. Cox, W. M. "Slow Learners Have a Normal Interest Span," *Clearing House*, 26:472–473 (April, 1952).

95. Eisman, Louis, Lawrence H. Feigenbaum, Ralph Freyer, and Louis A. Schuker. "The Slow Learner in the High School," *High Points*, 37:11–31 (April, 1955).

96. Farran, W. W. "Can you Pick the Dropouts?" *Texas Outlook*, 49:34–35 (January, 1965).

97. Featherstone, William B. "What Do We Know about Slow Learners?" *Clearing House*, 25:323 (February, 1951).

98. Ferguson, Donald G. "Review of Literature on the Slow Learner," *Education*, 81:326–330 (February, 1961).

99. Johnson, G. Orville. "The Relationship of Learning Rate and Developmental Rate," *Exceptional Child*, 26:68 (October, 1959).

100. Liddle, Gordon P. "Psychological Factors and the Dropout," *The High School Journal*, 45:276–280 (April, 1962).

101. Lightfoot, Georgia F. *Personality Characteristics of Bright and Dull Children.* New York: Teachers College Press, 1951. 136 pp.

102. New Jersey Secondary School Teachers Association. *The Slow Learner in Secondary Schools: 1961 Yearbook.* Plainfield, New Jersey: The Association, 1961. 100 pp.

103. Riessman, Frank. "Low Income Culture, the Adolescent, and the School," *National Association of Secondary School Principals Bulletin,* 49:45–49 (April, 1962).

104. Sorensen, Mourits A. "Low Ability Dropouts Versus Low Ability Graduates," *Personnel and Guidance Journal,* 39:144–145 (October, 1960).

105. Thomas, Harrison G. "The Walton High School XG Program," *High Points,* 32:20–54 (November, 1950).

EVALUATION

106. Baumeister, Alfred A. "Use of the W.I.S.C. with Mental Retardates: A Review," *American Journal of Mental Deficiency,* 69:183–194 (September, 1964).

107. Bellenger, Mary Ellen. "Guidance for the Disaffected," in "Disaffected Children and Youth," *Educational Leadership,* February, 1963.

108. Buros, Oscar Krisen (ed.) *The Sixth Mental Measurements Yearbook.* Highland Park, New Jersey: The Gryphon Press, 1965. 479 pp.

109. Clarke, A. D. B., and A. M. Clarke. "How Constant is the I.Q.?" *Lancet,* ii:877–880 (1953).

110. Deutsch, Martin, Jacob Fishman, Louis Kogan, Robert D. North, and M. Whiteman. "Guidelines for Testing Minority Group Children," *Journal of Social Issues,* 20:129–145 (March, 1964).

111. Kephart, Newell C. *The Slow Learner in the Classroom.* Columbus, Ohio: Charles E. Merrill, 1960. 292 pp.

112. Larson, Richard, and James L. Olson. "A Method of Identifying Culturally Deprived Kindergarten Children," *Exceptional Children,* 30:130–134 (November, 1963).

113. Lawson, John R., and Donald Avila. "Comparison of Wide Range Achievement Test and Gray Oral Reading Paragraphs Reading Scores of Mentally Retarded Adults," *Perceptual and Motor Skills,* 14:474–476 (June, 1962).

114. McCandless, Boyd. "Environment and Intelligence," *American Journal of Mental Deficiency,* 56:674–691 (April, 1952).

115. Nickel, Kenneth. "Better Education for Non-academic Pupils," *North Central Association Quarterly,* 31:352–384 (April, 1957).

116. Pate, John E. "Screening Beginning First Graders for Potential Problems," *Exceptional Children,* 32:111 (October, 1965).

CURRICULUM

117. Baynham, Dorsey. "The Great Cities Project," *National Education Association Journal,* 52:17–20 (April, 1963).

118. Brittain, Clay V. "Preschool Programs for Culturally Deprived Children," *Children,* 13:130–134 (July–August, 1966).

119. Champaign Public Schools. "The Efficacy of a Prevocational Curriculum and Services Designed to Rehabilitate Slow Learners Who Are School Drop Out, Delinquency, and Unemployment Prone," Champaign, Illinois: Champaign Community Unit Four Schools, Vocational Rehabilitation Administration, RD-1075-P, 1964 report. Mimeographed.

120. Connor, Frances P., and Mabel E. Talbot. *An Experimental Curriculum for Young Mentally Retarded Children.* New York: Teachers College Press, 1964. 300 pp.

121. Davey, Edward J. "Provide the Tools: a basic program for the nonacademic pupil," *Clearing House,* 39:351–352 (February, 1965).

122. Davis, Frank J. "Basics: classes in basic skills," *Texas Outlook,* 48:31–34 (September, 1964).

123. Deutsch, Martin. "Early Social Environment: Its Influence on School Adaptation," *The School Dropout,* D. Schreiber (ed.), Washington, D.C.: National Education Association, 1964, pp. 89–100.

124. Edwards, Rosaline M. "A Slow Learner Program," *National Association of Secondary School Principals Bulletin,* 40:130–134 (February, 1958).

125. Everitt, Donald, et al. "Careful Planning Creates New Vistas for Slow Learners," *Clearing House,* 37:8–10 (September, 1962).

126. Featherstone, William B. *Teaching the Slow Learner,* rev. ed. New York: Teachers College Press, 1951. 118 pp.

127. Fouracre, Maurice H., Frances P. Connor, and I. Ignacy Goldberg. *The Effects of a Preschool Program Upon Young Educable Mentally Retarded Children,* Volume I: Measurable Growth and Development Project Report on Project No. AE 6444, Washington, D.C.: U.S. Office of Education, 1962. 128 pp.

128. Herkner, M. W., and J. F. Malone. "How Shall We Provide for the Slow Learner in Junior High School?" *National Association of Secondary School Principals Bulletin,* 38:95–100 (April, 1954).

129. Medford Public Schools. "Revised Instructional Program for 'Slow-Learners' to Improve Their Job Placement Opportunities: A

Three Phase Study," OE-5-85-010 Progress Report, Medford, Oregon: Medford Public Schools, March, 1966. Mimeographed.

130. Medina Central School District No. 1. "Pre-Vocational World History Curriculum, Grade 10; Pre-Vocational Social Studies Curriculum, Grade 9," Medina, New York: Medina Public Schools, 1964. Mimeographed.

131. Melby, Ernest D. (quoted in) *Phi Delta Kappan,* 46:449 (May, 1965).

132. National Education Association. "Education of the Slow Learner," *N.E.A. Research Memo. 18,* Washington, D.C.: National Education Association, Research Division, 1964. 6 pp.

133. Pellman, Maurine, and Gordon P. Liddle. "A Program for the Problem Child," *Phi Delta Kappan,* 40:174–178 (January, 1959).

134. Philadelphia Public Schools. *The Key to Teaching Slow Learners in the High School.* Philadelphia: Curriculum Office, Philadelphia Public Schools, 1959.

135. Quincy Public Schools and Southern Illinois University. "An Educational Program for Slow Learners in Grades 7 through 12," Quincy, Illinois: Quincy Public Schools and Southern Illinois University, 1964. Mimeographed.

136. Robinson, Donald W. "Scraps from a Teacher's Notebook," *Phi Delta Kappan,* 47:102 (October, 1965).

137. ———. "Head Starts in Mississippi," *Phi Delta Kappan,* 47:91–95 (October, 1965).

138. Rochester Public Schools. *A Suggested Program for Slow Learners, Secondary Schools.* Rochester, New York: Board of Education, 1958.

139. Savitzsky, Charles. "Introduction to a Program for Possible Dropouts," *High Points,* 43:5–9 (November, 1961).

140. Seeley, R. M. "A Junior High Core Program for Slow Learners," *School Executive,* 73:64–66 (October, 1953).

141. Shawn, Bernard. "Even the Slow Must Start," *New York State Education,* 52:8–9 (December, 1964).

142. Smith, B. Othaneal, William Stanley, and Harlan J. Shores. *Fundamentals of Curriculum Development.* New York: World Book Company, 1957. 685 pp.

143. Spacks, Barry. "How to Learn a Secret Name," *American Education,* 1:7–12 (June, 1965).

144. Stratemeyer, Florence, Hamden Forkner, Margaret McKim, and

A. Harry Passow. *Developing a Curriculum for Modern Living,* 2nd ed. New York: Teachers College Press, 1957. 740 pp.

145. Strauss, Alfred A., and Laura Lehtinen. *Psychopathology and Education of the Brain Injured Child,* Vol. I, New York: Grune and Stratton, 1947. 206 pp.

146. Strauss, Alfred A., and Newell C. Kephart. *Psychopathology and Education of the Brain Injured Child,* Vol. II, New York: Grune and Stratton, 1955. 266 pp.

147. Sudlow, Robert E. "A Survey of the Research and Literature on the Slow Learner and Its Application to the Prevocational Program in the Secondary Schools of Medina," Medina, New York: Medina Public Schools, 1965. Mimeographed.

148. Talbot, Mabel. *Box Books,* Council Bluffs, Iowa: Box Books, 1410 Long View Drive, 1966.

149. Thorsell, Marguerite. "Organizing Experience Units for Educable Mentally Retarded," *Exceptional Children,* 28:177–186 (December, 1961).

150. Tucker, Ruel E. "A Program for Slow Learners," *National Association of Secondary School Principals Bulletin,* 36:333–337 (March, 1952).

151. Tutton, Marie E. "A Total School Approach to the Slow Learner," *Clearing House,* 37:434–439 (March, 1963).

ART, FINE AND APPLIED

152. Dick, Arthur A. "What Can Be Done for Slow Learners in Industrial Arts?" *Industrial Arts and Vocational Education,* 46:117–119, April, 1957.

153. Moeller, Charles A. "Slow Learner: Meeting the Challenge," *High School Journal,* 46:285–290, May, 1963.

154. Venable, Margaret. "High School Dumping Grounds," *School Arts,* 63:32–34, May, 1964.

BUSINESS EDUCATION

155. Austin, Richard L. "A Method of Using the Bookkeeping Practice Set to Aid the Slow Learner," *Balance Sheet,* 40:393–401 (May, 1959).

156. Brown, Eleanor. "They Can't Learn? Don't Believe It," *Business Education World,* 40:15–17 (November, 1959).

157. Calhoun, Calfrey C. "Challenge of the Slow Learner," *Business Education Forum*, 17:25–27 (May, 1963).

158. Crawfis, Janice E. "The Slow Learner in Business Education," *Journal of Business Education*, 40: Part I, 19–20 (October, 1965); Part II, 65–67 (November, 1965).

159. Ellenbogen, Allen. "How to Teach Clerical Practice to Slow Learners," *Business Education World*, 44:26 (April, 1964).

160. Eyster, Elvin S. "Preparing the Lower One-third in General Scholastic Ability for Business Employment," *Journal of Business Education*, 39:180–181 (February, 1964).

161. Feather, James R. "Meeting the Individual Differences in Typewriting," *Journal of Business Education*, 34:125–126 (December, 1958).

162. Haga, Enoch J. "Simplify Bookkeeping for Your Slow Learners," *Business Education World*, 41:12–13 (February, 1961).

163. Henderson, Braxton. "Bookkeeping and the Low-ability Student," *Balance Sheet*, 44:251–252 (February, 1963).

164. House, F. Wayne. "Are You Solving the Reading Problem in Bookkeeping?" *Business Education World*, 33:291–292 (February, 1953).

165. Krawitz, Myron J. "The Case of the Reluctant Learners," *Business Education World*, 40:19–21 (November, 1959).

166. ———. "Let's Find Some Square Holes," *Business Education World*, 45:19–23 (October, 1964).

167. Perry, Enose, Maxie Lee Work, Dorothy Schwartz, Hazel Flood, Margaret Andrews, and Harlund Samson. "Symposium—Business Education for Students of Lower Ability," *Business Education Forum*, 14:30–34 (January, 1960).

168. Plymire, Boyd G. "Integrating Slower and Faster Beginning Typists," *Journal of Business Education*, 33:350–352 (May, 1958).

169. Rothchild, Thomas A. "Business Education and the Slow Learner," *Balance Sheet*, 47:104–108 (November, 1965).

170. Satlow, I. David. "Graded Materials for the Slow Learner in Bookkeeping," *Journal of Business Education*, 20:22–24 (October, 1944).

171. Shotak, Rosalyn. "Helping the Slower Shorthand Students," *Business Teacher*, 36:25–26 (April, 1959).

172. Shows, Velma. "Clerical Practice for the Slow Learner," *Journal of Business Education*, 31:17–18 (October, 1955).

173. University of the State of New York. *Suggestions for Teaching Business Pupils of Different Ability Levels—with Special Emphasis on Pupils Experiencing Difficulty.* Albany, New York: Bureau of Business and Distributive Education, State Education Department, 1964. 44 pp.

174. Wolters, Carl E. (Jr.). "Individual Differences in Bookkeeping," *Business Education World,* 43:7–8 (October, 1962).

COMMUNICATION SKILLS

175. Alexander, Erin. "English Has Been—," *English Journal,* 52:102–104 (February, 1963).

176. California State Committee on Developmental Reading. "Suggestions for Teaching Slow Learners," *National Association of Secondary School Principals Bulletin,* 35:23–42 (February, 1951).

177. Clark, Marie B. "Grouping Helps Children Succeed in the Intermediate Grades," in *Readings on Reading Instruction,* Albert J. Harris (ed.), New York: David McKay, 1963. 425 pp.

178. Ebbitt, Paul F. "Drama for Slow Learners," *English Journal,* 52:624–626 (November, 1963).

179. Epler, M. R., and O. B. Handley, "Third Group Pupil," *Elementary School Journal,* 59:451–453 (May, 1959).

180. Gates, Arthur I., and M. C. Pritchard. "Teaching Reading to Slow-Learning or 'Dull-Normal' Pupils," *Teachers College Record,* 43:255–263 (January, 1942).

181. Goldberg, Milton. "My Slow Learners' New I.Q.: Imagination Quotient," *Clearing House,* 28:337–340 (February, 1954).

182. Goldstein, Herbert, and Rick F. Heber. "A Note on Research," in *Preparation of Mentally Retarded Youth for Gainful Employment,* Romaine P. Mackie (ed.), Washington, D.C.: Government Printing Office, 1959. 86 pp.

183. Greene, Jay E. "A 'Slow English Class' Investigates Community Living," *English Journal,* 40:339–341 (June, 1951).

184. Justa, Sister Mary. "Meeting the Reading Needs of the Slow Learners," *Journal of Education,* 137:11–15 (October, 1954).

185. Keyes, George E. "Creative Dramatics and the Slow Learner," *English Journal,* 54:81–84 (February, 1965).

186. Kirk, Samuel A. *Teaching Reading to Slow Learning Children.* Boston: Houghton Mifflin Co., 1940. 225 pp.

187. Lee, Doris M., and Robert Van Allen. *Learning to Read Through Experience.* New York: Appleton-Century-Crofts, 1963. 146 pp.

188. Leo, Sister Mary. "English for the Non-Academic Student," *Catholic School Journal,* 64:64–65 (September, 1964).

189. Lessem, Stanley W. "Reading for Slow Learners," *English Journal,* 45:275–277 (May, 1956).

190. Leven, L. M. "Projects in English Class Can Help Solve Student's Problems," *Business Education World,* 45:17–19 (September, 1964).

191. Lobdell, Lawrence O. "A Classic as Reading Material for Retarded Readers," *English Journal,* 39:491–495 (June, 1950).

192. McCarthy, William, and Joan Oliver. "Some Tactile-kinesthetic Procedures for Teaching Reading to Slow Learning Children," *Exceptional Children,* 31:419–421 (April, 1965).

193. McElravy, Anna. "Handwriting and the Slow Learner," *Elementary English,* 41:865–868 (December, 1964).

194. New Jersey Association of Teachers of English. *Kit of Materials for the Slow Learner in English.* New Brunswick: The Association, 1964. 34 pp. Mimeographed.

195. Pritchett, Ada Anthis. "Aliveness—Then Retention," *Elementary English,* 38:581–583 (December, 1961).

196. Ross, Frank E. "For the Disadvantaged Student: A Program that Swings," *English Journal,* 54:280–283 (April, 1965).

197. Schonell, Fred J. *The Psychology of Teaching Reading* (4th ed.). New York: The Philosophical Library, 1962. 295 pp.

198. Shehan, Lawrence P. "Reaching Slow Learners," *English Journal,* 51:44–46 (January, 1962).

199. Sierles, Samuel. "The Slow Learner Can Learn!" *Clearing House,* 36:361–363 (February, 1962).

200. Stahlecker, Lotar V. "Motivating the Slow Learner to Read," *High School Journal,* 46:78–82 (December, 1962).

201. Strang, Ruth, Constance M. McCullough, and Arthur E. Traxler. *The Improvement of Reading.* New York: McGraw-Hill, 1961. 359 pp.

202. Strang, Ruth. "Out of the Classroom: Step by Step Instruction in Beginning Reading for Slow Learners," *Exceptional Children,* 32:31–36 (September, 1965).

203. Sullivan, Helen B. "Skills Instruction for the Slow-learning Child in the Regular Classroom," *National Elementary Principal,* 29:41–46 (December, 1949).

204. Thorson, Robert M. "In Slow Gear—Drama without Tears," *Instructor,* 75:44 (December, 1965).

205. Tincher, Ethel. "Helping Slow Learners Achieve Success," *English Journal,* 54:289–294 (April, 1963).

206. Yarborough, Betty H. "Teaching English to Slow Learners," *Teacher's Notebook in English,* New York: Harcourt, Brace, and World, Spring, 1962. 6 pp.

207. Zamchick, David. "The Battle of the Book: Slow Learners," *Clearing House,* 33:41–43 (September, 1958).

HOME AND FAMILY-LIFE EDUCATION

208. Denton, L. H., and L. E. Hoffman. "Family Arts: A Course for Slow-Learning Junior High School Girls," *National Association of Secondary School Principals Bulletin,* 25:81–84 (April, 1941).

209. Fernandez, Louise. *The Slow Learner in Homemaking Education,* D.H.E. Topics #10, Washington, D.C.: The Department of Home Economics, National Education Association, no date. 15 pp.

210. Fleck, Henrietta. "Teaching the Slow Learner," *Practical Forecast for Home Economics,* 10:13–15 (October, 1964).

MATHEMATICS EDUCATION

211. Adkins, Julia. "Kit for Arithmetic," *Arithmetic Teacher,* 7:252–253 (May, 1960).

212. Adler, Irving. "Mathematics for the Low Achiever," *NEA Journal,* 54:28–30 (February, 1965).

213. Berndt, Trudy. "Classroom Arithmetic Kit," *Instructor,* 72:22–24 (January, 1963).

214. Bridges, Raymond. "Easily Made Arithmetic Aids," *Arithmetic Teacher,* 10:507–509 (December, 1963).

215. Fehr, Howard. "Modern Mathematics and Good Pedagogy," *Arithmetic Teacher,* 10:402–411 (November, 1963).

216. Greenholz, Sarah. "What's New in Teaching Slow Learners in Junior High School?" *Mathematics Teacher,* 52:522–528 (December, 1964).

217. Groenendyk, Eldert A. "Use of Calculators in Teaching Mathematics," Pella, Iowa: Central University of Iowa Press, no date. 2 pp. Mimeographed.

218. ——— and Terry E. Shoemaker. *Experimental Ninth Grade General Mathematics Teacher Handbook.* Pella, Iowa: Central University of Iowa Press, 1966. 87 pp.

219. Holinger, Dorothy. "Helping the Non-Learner in Grade One," *Arithmetic Teacher,* 5:15–24 (February, 1958).

220. Jacobs, James N., Joan Bollenbacher, and Mildred Keiffer. "Teaching Seventh-Grade Mathematics by Television to Homogeneously Grouped Below-Average Pupils," *Mathematics Teacher,* 54:551–555 (November, 1961).

221. Kovinow, Muriel C. "Live Insurance: An Experience for Slow Learners," *High Points,* 46:55–58 (January, 1964).

222. Krulik, Stephen. "Experiences with Some Different Topics for the Slow Learner," *National Association of Secondary School Principals Bulletin,* 43:43–46 (May, 1959).

223. ———. *The Use of Concepts in Mathematics, New in Teaching the Slow Learner,* Ed.D. Project, Teachers College, Columbia University, 1961.

224. Lerch, H. H., and Francis J. Kelly. "A Mathematics Program for Slow Learners at the Junior High Level," *Arithmetic Teacher,* 13:232–236 (March, 1966).

225. Parrish, Cada R. "Fun, Fact and Fancy," *Arithmetic Teacher,* 11:39–41 (January, 1964).

226. Potter, Mary, and Virgil Mallory. *Education in Mathematics for the Slow Learner.* Washington, D.C.: National Council of Teachers of Mathematics, 1958. 36 pp.

227. Proctor, Amelia D. "World of Hope: Helping Slow Learners Enjoy Mathematics," *Mathematics Teacher,* 58:118–122 (February, 1965).

228. Rasmussen, Love. "Countering Cultural Deprivation Via the Elementary Mathematics Library," in *The Low Achiever in Mathematics,* Lauren G. Woodby (ed.), Washington, D.C.: Government Printing Office, 1965. 96 pp.

229. Rosenbloom, Paul (ed.). *C.A.M.P. Project Conference Report, April, 1966.* Pella, Iowa: Central College, 1966. 53 pp.

230. School Mathematics Study Group. *Conference on Mathematics Education for Below Average Achievers.* Pasadena, California: Vroman's, 1964. 130 pp.

231. Sobel, Max A. "Providing for the Slow Learner in the Junior High School," *Mathematics Teacher,* 52:347–353 (May, 1959).

232. Willerding, Margaret F. "The Use of Graphs for Retarded Children," *Arithmetic Teacher,* 4:258–261 (December, 1957).

233. Woodby, Lauren G. (ed.). *The Low Achiever in Mathematics.* Washington, D.C.: Government Printing Office, 1965. 98 pp.

MUSIC EDUCATION

234. Newacheck, Vivian. "Music and the Slow Learner," *Music Educator's Journal,* 40:50–53 (November, 1963).

235. Nye, Robert E. (ed.). *Music for Elementary School Children.* Washington, D.C.: The Center for Applied Research in Education, Inc., 1963. 397 pp.

236. Petzold, Robert G. "The Development of Auditory Perception of Musical Sounds by Children in the First Six Grades," in *Music for Elementary School Children,* Robert E. Nye (ed.), Washington, D.C.: The Center for Applied Research in Education, Inc., 1965. 397 pp.

237. Sur, William, and Charles F. Schuller. *Music Education for Teen-Agers,* 2nd ed., New York: Harper & Row, 1966. 363 pp.

SCIENCE EDUCATION

238. Ennis, Joseph. "Course in Applied Science for Non-Academic Pupils and Slow Learners," *High Points,* 32:50–55 (February, 1950).

239. Lichtenstein, Ruth J. "Teaching Biology to the Slow Learner," *High Points,* 47:59–62 (April, 1965).

240. Liebherr, Harold G., and Glen E. Peterson (eds.). *The Teacher and BSCS Special Materials.* Boulder, Colorado: Biological Sciences Curriculum Study, 1966. 70 pp.

241. Moore, Arnold J. "Science Instructional Materials for the Low-Ability Junior High School Student," *School Science and Mathematics,* 62:556–559 (November, 1962).

242. Rudman, Soloman. "A Special Science Curriculum: A Course of Study for the Retarded and Slow Students in the Secondary Schools," *Clearing House,* 37:114–117 (October, 1962).

SOCIAL STUDIES EDUCATION

243. Abramowitz, Jack. "Revolutionizing the Teaching of the Social Studies to the Slow Learner," *Social Education,* 23:219–222 (May, 1959).

244. Bolzau, Elios L. "Adapting American History to Slow Learners," *Social Education,* 14:115–120 (March, 1950).

245. D'Ambrosio, Louis M. "Adjusting the Social Studies to the Non-Academically Inclined Child," *High Points,* 34:13–18 (January, 1952).

246. Fenton, Edwin (ed.). *Teaching the New Social Studies in Secondary Schools: An Inductive Approach.* New York: Holt, Rinehart, and Winston, 1966. 526 pp.

247. Helburn, Nicholas. "Improving Communication Between the Teacher and the Geographer: The Role of the High School Geography Project," *The Journal of Geography,* 64:149–153 (April, 1965).

248. Herman, A. "Current Events for the Slow Learner," *High Points,* 35:31–35 (November, 1953).

249. Koch, Conrad. "Helping the Slow Learner," *High Points,* 45:67–69 (June, 1963).

250. Kohn, Clyde F. (ed.). *Selected Classroom Experiences: High School Geography Project.* Normal, Illinois: Publications Center, National Council for Geographic Education, 1964. 59 pp.

251. Koob, M. L. "Using Newspaper Editorials in Slow Classes," *High Points,* 44:54–56 (January, 1962).

252. McFeely, R. H. "Faculty Planning to Meet Individual Differences: for the Slow Learner," *National Council for Social Studies,* 15th Yearbook, 1944.

253. Miller, Jemima, and Grace Weston. "Slow Learners Improve in Critical Thinking," *Social Education,* 13:315–319 (November, 1949).

254. Peller, Helen. "Adjusting in Adjustment Class," *High Points,* 29:72–78 (April, 1947).

255. Switzer, W. J. "Secondary Course in World Geography and the Slow Learner," *Journal of Geography,* 63:169–174 (April, 1964).